Artificial Intelligence for Web Development

Using AI for Efficient Web Applications

Hedwig Garrett

Table of Contents

Artificial Intelligence for Web Development: Using AI for Efficient Web Applications

Chapter 5: AI-Powered Chatbots and Virtual Assistants

- Understanding AI Chatbots for Websites
- Using Dialogflow, OpenAI, and IBM Watson for Chatbot Development
- Implementing AI Chatbots in JavaScript and Python
- Improving Customer Experience with AI-Powered Support Systems

Chapter 6: AI-Based Content Generation and SEO Optimization

- How AI Enhances Content Creation and Blogging
- AI-Powered SEO Tools: Google BERT, Surfer SEO, and Clearscope
- AI-Driven Keyword Research and SEO Audits
- Automating Content Optimization for Search Engines

SECTION 3: AI-Powered Backend Web Development

Chapter 7: Automating Backend Processes with AI

- AI for Data Processing and Form Validation
- AI-Driven CRUD Operations and Database Management
- How AI Helps in Automating Backend Workflows

Chapter 8: AI for Web Security and Threat Detection

- AI in Cybersecurity for Web Applications
- Machine Learning Models for Detecting Threats
- AI-Based Fraud Prevention and Spam Detection

Chapter 9: AI-Powered Search and Recommendation Systems

- AI-Driven Search Algorithms for Web Applications
- Implementing Elasticsearch with AI Enhancements
- Building AI-Powered Recommendation Systems for E-Commerce

SECTION 4: AI and Web Application Deployment

Chapter 10: AI-Powered Performance Optimization

- AI for Web Speed and Performance Enhancement
- AI-Based Image and Video Compression

- Machine Learning for Predicting Server Load

Chapter 11: AI in Cloud and Serverless Web Development

- AI-Powered DevOps for CI/CD Automation
- Leveraging AI in AWS, Google Cloud, and Azure AI
- Integrating AI in Serverless Web Applications

Chapter 12: Ethical Considerations and Challenges in AI Web Development

- Bias and Fairness in AI Web Applications
- Privacy and Security Concerns in AI-Powered Websites
- Compliance with GDPR, CCPA, and Other Regulations

SECTION 5: Hands-On AI Web Development Projects

Chapter 13: Building an AI-Powered Chatbot for a Website

- Designing a Chatbot Using OpenAI and Python/JavaScript
- Deploying the Chatbot in a Web Application
- Enhancing the Chatbot with Machine Learning

Chapter 14: Implementing AI-Based Image Recognition in a Web App

- Using TensorFlow.js for Image Classification
- Deploying an AI-Powered Image Recognition Tool on a Website
- Enhancing Web Security with AI-Based Facial Recognition

Chapter 15: Creating an AI-Powered Recommendation System

- Building a Personalized Recommendation Engine
- Implementing AI Recommendations in E-Commerce Web Apps
- Testing and Optimizing AI-Powered Recommendations

Chapter 16: Automating SEO with AI

- Using AI for Automated Keyword Analysis
- Developing an AI-Driven Web Performance Analyzer
- Deploying an AI-Based SEO Optimization System

Final Thoughts

- Key Takeaways from AI-Driven Web Development
- The Future of AI in Web Development
- Recommended Resources for Further Learning

Chapter 1

Introduction to AI for Web Applications

The Evolution of AI in Web Development

Early Web Development: Static Websites and Basic Interactions

The internet's early days were characterized by simple, static websites built using **HTML** and **CSS**. These websites were nothing more than digital brochures, displaying static information with minimal user interaction. The role of a developer was limited to designing pages that provided content but lacked any form of **intelligence or automation**.

During this period, web applications were **purely reactive**, meaning they only displayed content that was manually updated. There was **no real-time interaction**, no predictive analytics, and certainly no concept of **artificial intelligence** improving the user experience.

Even as JavaScript was introduced in the mid-1990s, allowing for **dynamic interactions**, AI was still far from being incorporated into mainstream web development. Instead, most enhancements focused on improving user interface elements rather than introducing any form of automation or intelligence.

The Advent of Data-Driven Web Applications

As the internet matured, so did the **expectations of users**. Businesses realized that a simple static page was not enough. This led to the rise of **database-driven web applications**, powered by technologies like **PHP, MySQL, and ASP.NET**. Websites could now store user data, process requests dynamically, and provide **personalized content**.

During this period, companies like **Amazon and Google** revolutionized web applications by leveraging **big data** to analyze user behavior. Although this was not yet **AI-powered**, it laid the foundation for **machine learning-based recommendation systems** that would later become an essential component of AI-driven web development.

This was the time when search engines like **Google began using algorithms** to provide relevant search results based on **keywords and backlinks**. However, AI's role was still minimal, and most websites functioned based on **predefined rules and static queries**.

Rise of Machine Learning in Web Applications

The real shift toward **AI in web development** started in the early 2010s, when machine learning models became more accessible to developers. Companies began integrating **AI-driven analytics** to track user interactions and automate processes.

Several key developments during this time include:

- **Chatbots**: Early AI-driven chatbots emerged, enabling automated customer support on websites.
- **Recommendation Engines**: Companies like Amazon and Netflix began leveraging machine learning to suggest content based on user preferences.
- **Search Engine Intelligence**: Google's **RankBrain** AI started improving search result accuracy by understanding **user intent** rather than just matching keywords.

The integration of AI into web development became more apparent as developers started using **natural language processing (NLP)** and **computer vision** for interactive applications.

The Era of AI-Powered Web Development

Today, AI is deeply integrated into web applications, transforming how users interact with digital platforms. Several modern AI-driven enhancements include:

1. **Personalization Engines**: AI predicts user behavior and tailors experiences dynamically.
2. **Automated UI/UX Design**: AI-driven tools adjust layouts, colors, and fonts to optimize engagement.

3. **AI-Powered Chatbots**: Websites now feature **advanced virtual assistants** capable of handling customer queries without human intervention.
4. **Predictive Search & Auto-Completion**: AI enhances web search experiences by predicting user queries before they are typed completely.
5. **Cybersecurity & Fraud Detection**: AI-powered systems **detect anomalies**, preventing data breaches and fraudulent activities.

The evolution of AI in web development has **shifted the role of developers** from simply coding static applications to integrating **intelligent, automated, and predictive functionalities** that enhance user experience and business operations.

How AI is Transforming Modern Websites

1. AI-Driven Personalization

AI has **completely changed** how websites deliver content to users. Modern AI-powered algorithms track **user behavior, preferences, and past interactions** to create a highly personalized experience.

Examples of AI-Powered Personalization:

- **E-Commerce Platforms**: Websites like **Amazon and eBay** use AI to **recommend products** based on past purchases and browsing behavior.
- **Streaming Services**: **Netflix, YouTube, and Spotify** analyze user behavior to suggest content that aligns with their preferences.
- **News Websites**: Platforms like **Google News and Apple News** curate articles based on a user's reading history and interests.

AI ensures that every visitor gets a **customized experience**, increasing user engagement and retention rates.

---

2. AI-Powered Chatbots and Virtual Assistants

One of the biggest AI-driven innovations in web development is the integration of **chatbots and virtual assistants**. Traditional customer support methods required human representatives, but AI-powered bots can now handle **thousands of queries simultaneously** with high accuracy.

How AI Chatbots Are Transforming Websites:

- **24/7 Availability**: AI-powered chatbots provide instant responses at any time, eliminating the need for human intervention.
- **Natural Language Processing (NLP)**: Chatbots now **understand human language**, making conversations more natural and efficient.
- **E-Commerce Integration**: Bots help customers find products, track orders, and handle complaints without requiring a customer support agent.

Websites that utilize AI-powered customer service **improve user satisfaction**, reduce **response times**, and **boost engagement**.

---

3. AI in Web Security and Fraud Prevention

Cybersecurity is a major concern for **modern websites**, and AI plays a critical role in identifying and preventing cyber threats.

AI's Role in Web Security:

- **Fraud Detection**: AI systems analyze transactions to detect fraudulent activities in **real-time**.
- **Anomaly Detection**: Machine learning models track website traffic and identify **suspicious activities**.
- **Automated Threat Response**: AI detects and **neutralizes** cyber threats before they cause damage.

For example, AI-powered **captcha verification systems** can now determine whether a user is a **human or a bot** by analyzing behavior rather than relying on traditional text-based CAPTCHAs.

---

4. AI-Powered Search and Smart Recommendations

Modern websites now use **AI-powered search engines** that deliver **faster, more relevant** results based on **user intent rather than keywords**.

AI in Web Search and Recommendations:

- **Google's AI-Powered Search Algorithms**: Google's **RankBrain and BERT AI models** analyze search queries to improve result accuracy.

- **E-Commerce Search Engines**: Websites like **Amazon and eBay** use AI-driven search tools that show the **most relevant products** to users.
- **AI-Powered Content Recommendations**: News platforms and blogs use AI to recommend articles based on user preferences.

This AI-driven approach improves the **overall efficiency** of web applications, ensuring users find exactly what they need in less time.

---

5. AI-Enhanced Web Performance Optimization

Website **performance and speed** play a crucial role in **user experience and SEO rankings**. AI is now being used to **automatically optimize website performance** without manual intervention.

AI-Driven Performance Enhancements:

- **AI-Based Caching Strategies**: AI predicts which web pages users will visit next and preloads them to reduce load times.
- **Real-Time Resource Allocation**: AI dynamically adjusts server resources based on traffic spikes to prevent downtime.
- **AI-Optimized Image Compression**: AI automatically compresses images and videos to reduce **page load times** without sacrificing quality.

This ensures that websites remain **fast, responsive, and user-friendly**, even under heavy traffic loads.

---

6. AI in Web Design and Development Automation

AI has also revolutionized the way websites are **designed and developed**. Automated **AI-driven website builders** and **design assistants** can now create visually appealing web pages **without human intervention**.

AI Tools Transforming Web Development:

- **Adobe Sensei**: Uses AI to automate design processes.
- **Wix ADI (Artificial Design Intelligence)**: Creates websites based on user input.
- **Figma AI Plugins**: Suggests design improvements based on industry trends.

By automating web design, AI **reduces development time, enhances creativity, and ensures data-driven decision-making**.

AI is no longer a futuristic concept—it is actively transforming **every aspect of web development**. From **personalized user experiences and AI-driven search engines** to **automated security measures and intelligent design tools**, AI is making web applications **smarter, faster, and more efficient**. As technology continues to evolve, AI will play an even greater role in **shaping the future of web development**.

AI vs Traditional Programming: Key Differences

The fundamental difference between **Artificial Intelligence (AI) programming** and **traditional programming** lies in how they approach problem-solving. Traditional programming is **rule-based**, where a developer writes explicit instructions for the computer to follow. AI programming, on the other hand, involves systems that learn from data, adapt to new inputs, and improve over time.

To better understand these differences, let's explore key aspects where AI and traditional programming diverge.

---

1. Rule-Based vs. Learning-Based Systems

- **Traditional Programming:**

    - Follows a strict set of rules predefined by developers.
    - Requires step-by-step instructions to perform a task.
    - Cannot adapt to new data unless explicitly reprogrammed.
- **AI-Based Programming:**

    - Learns patterns from data using **machine learning (ML) algorithms**.
    - Adjusts its behavior dynamically based on experience.
    - Can handle uncertain or unstructured data more effectively.

Example:
A **traditional spam filter** relies on **predefined rules** (e.g., blocking emails with specific keywords like "lottery" or "win money"). An **AI-powered spam filter** analyzes

email patterns, learns from user behavior, and continuously updates itself based on new spam trends.

2. Deterministic vs. Probabilistic Output

- **Traditional Programming:**

  - Produces **consistent, predictable** results when given the same inputs.
  - Works well for structured problems where outcomes are clearly defined.
- **AI-Based Programming:**

  - Produces **probabilistic outputs**, meaning it assigns a likelihood to different possible answers.
  - Can make errors or change results over time as it learns from new data.

Example:
A traditional **weather forecasting program** calculates expected temperatures using **predefined formulas** based on historical data. An **AI-powered weather model** analyzes large datasets, learns from patterns, and predicts temperature changes dynamically with **probability scores**.

3. Data Dependency and Adaptability

- **Traditional Programming:**

  - Works efficiently when problems have **static, well-defined rules**.
  - Requires developers to update the program manually whenever new rules are needed.
- **AI-Based Programming:**

  - Relies on **large datasets** to identify patterns and make predictions.
  - Continuously adapts as it is fed **new, real-world data**.

Example:
A traditional **recommendation system** (e.g., on an e-commerce site) suggests products based on **preset categories**. An AI-based system like **Amazon's**
7

recommendation engine analyzes real-time purchase history, browsing behavior, and global trends to recommend products dynamically.

---

4. Error Handling and Debugging

- **Traditional Programming:**

  - Errors arise due to **syntax mistakes or logical missteps** in predefined rules.
  - Debugging involves manually fixing errors based on clearly defined rules.
- **AI-Based Programming:**

  - Errors occur due to **incorrect data interpretations, biases, or overfitting**.
  - Debugging is complex because the AI model adjusts itself based on training data rather than following explicit rules.

Example:
In a **banking fraud detection system**, a traditional program checks for fraud based on predefined rules (e.g., flagging transactions above a certain amount). AI-powered fraud detection analyzes **millions of transactions**, detects anomalies, and **learns** over time to identify new fraudulent patterns.

---

5. Performance and Scalability

- **Traditional Programming:**

  - Performs well for **structured, small-scale problems**.
  - Struggles with handling **large datasets** or complex scenarios.
- **AI-Based Programming:**

  - Efficient at processing **large amounts of data** and recognizing complex patterns.
  - Can scale across multiple industries, from healthcare to finance and e-commerce.

Example:
A **manual customer support ticketing system** assigns queries to agents based on

8

predefined rules. AI-powered **chatbots and support assistants** process thousands of queries simultaneously, analyze conversation tone, and suggest **context-aware responses**.

---

6. Human Involvement in Decision-Making

- **Traditional Programming:**

    - Requires **continuous manual intervention** for new cases.
    - Decisions are **hardcoded**, meaning new scenarios need new programming.
- **AI-Based Programming:**

    - **Automates decision-making** based on learned data patterns.
    - Reduces human involvement by **self-improving over time**.

Example:
 A traditional **inventory management system** alerts store owners when stock levels are low, requiring human input for restocking. An **AI-powered inventory system** predicts demand fluctuations, suggests restocking schedules, and automatically places orders when needed.

Practical Applications of AI in Web Development

AI has **revolutionized** web development by automating tasks, improving user experiences, and enhancing website functionalities. Below are some key AI applications in modern web applications.

---

1. AI-Powered Chatbots and Virtual Assistants

- Enhance customer interactions by **providing instant responses**.
- Reduce workload for human support agents.
- Understand **natural language queries** using **NLP (Natural Language Processing)**.

Examples:

- **ChatGPT-based assistants** for handling **customer inquiries** on websites.
- **Facebook Messenger bots** that suggest products or answer FAQs.

---

2. AI-Driven Personalization and Recommendation Systems

- Customizes user experiences based on behavior.
- Increases engagement by delivering **relevant content or products**.
- Used in e-commerce, streaming platforms, and news websites.

Examples:

- **Netflix's AI algorithms** recommend movies based on viewing history.
- **Amazon suggests products** based on user browsing behavior.

---

3. AI-Powered Search and Auto-Suggestions

- Improves website search accuracy.
- Predicts user queries before they finish typing.
- Uses AI-based ranking to **prioritize the most relevant search results**.

Examples:

- **Google's AI-powered search algorithms** (RankBrain, BERT).
- **E-commerce smart search** that suggests products while typing.

---

4. AI in Web Security and Fraud Detection

- Identifies **unusual activities** to detect fraud.
- Monitors **website traffic patterns** for potential threats.
- Uses **AI-driven CAPTCHA systems** to distinguish humans from bots.

Examples:

- **PayPal's fraud detection AI** analyzing millions of transactions.
- **AI-powered CAPTCHA** systems that use behavioral tracking instead of text-based verification.

5. AI for Automated Web Development

- Auto-generates websites based on **user preferences**.
- Optimizes **UI/UX designs** based on behavior analytics.
- Reduces development time for web applications.

Examples:

- **Wix ADI (Artificial Design Intelligence)** creating websites automatically.
- **Adobe Sensei AI** optimizing design layouts.

Overview of AI Tools and Frameworks

Several AI tools and frameworks help developers integrate AI functionalities into web applications. Here are some essential ones:

1. Machine Learning Libraries

Tool	Description
TensorFlow .js	AI framework for web-based machine learning.
PyTorch	Deep learning framework widely used in AI research.
Scikit-Learn	Popular ML library for predictive modeling.
Keras	High-level deep learning framework based on TensorFlow.

2. NLP (Natural Language Processing) APIs

API	Use Case
Google NLP API	Sentiment analysis, entity recognition.
OpenAI GPT-4	AI-powered text generation, chatbots.
IBM Watson NLP	Text classification, speech-to-text.

3. AI-Powered Image Recognition

API	Function
Google Vision AI	Image recognition, OCR.
Amazon Rekognition	Face detection, image moderation.
OpenCV	Real-time image processing.

4. AI-Based Web Development Tools

Tool	Function
Wix ADI	AI-powered website builder.
Adobe Sensei	AI-driven design automation.
Google AutoML	Automated machine learning model training.

These tools help developers **integrate AI into web applications** efficiently, making AI-powered web development accessible to both beginners and experienced developers.

Chapter 2

Understanding Machine Learning for Web Development

Introduction to Machine Learning (ML)

Machine learning (ML) is a **subset of artificial intelligence (AI)** that enables computers to learn from data and make predictions or decisions without being explicitly programmed. Unlike traditional programming, where developers write specific rules to process inputs and generate outputs, ML models **identify patterns from data** and refine their predictions over time.

In web development, machine learning is revolutionizing how applications function, making them more **intelligent, efficient, and user-friendly**. From **personalized content recommendations** to **AI-powered search engines**, ML plays a crucial role in optimizing modern web applications.

How Machine Learning Works

At its core, machine learning follows a three-step process:

1. **Data Collection** – The system gathers **structured or unstructured data** from sources like user interactions, website logs, or third-party APIs.
2. **Training** – The ML model is trained on historical data, learning **patterns and relationships** between different variables.
3. **Prediction and Adaptation** – Once trained, the model applies its knowledge to **new data**, making predictions, adjusting its understanding, and continuously improving its accuracy.

These steps enable **self-learning** capabilities in web applications, allowing them to adapt based on user interactions and feedback.

Importance of Machine Learning in Web Development

Machine learning is widely used in web development for:

- **Personalization** – Websites analyze user behavior to **recommend content, products, or services** dynamically.
- **Search Optimization** – AI-driven search engines provide **more relevant** results using natural language processing (NLP).
- **Chatbots and Virtual Assistants** – AI-driven customer support systems **respond intelligently** to queries.
- **Fraud Detection** – Machine learning helps **identify suspicious activities** and prevent cyberattacks.
- **Automation** – AI automates complex backend processes, **reducing manual work**.

With the rise of **big data** and cloud computing, machine learning is becoming an **essential component** of modern web applications, transforming **user experiences, security, and performance**.

Supervised vs. Unsupervised vs. Reinforcement Learning

Machine learning is broadly categorized into **three types** based on how the model learns from data:

1. **Supervised Learning**
2. **Unsupervised Learning**
3. **Reinforcement Learning**

Each category serves different purposes in web development, from **predicting user preferences** to **detecting anomalies and optimizing website functionalities**.

---

1. Supervised Learning

Supervised learning is the most commonly used type of ML, where the model is trained using **labeled data**—meaning the input data is paired with the correct output. The system learns by mapping inputs to outputs and refining its predictions over time.

14

How Supervised Learning Works

1. **Training Data** – The dataset consists of **inputs (X) and corresponding outputs (Y)**.
2. **Learning Process** – The algorithm learns from the labeled dataset by identifying patterns.
3. **Prediction** – Once trained, the model predicts outputs for **new, unseen inputs**.
4. **Error Correction** – The model adjusts based on feedback to **improve accuracy**.

Supervised Learning Algorithms

Algorithm	Description	Use Case in Web Development
Linear Regression	Predicts continuous values.	Website load time prediction.
Logistic Regression	Classifies data into categories.	Spam detection in web forms.
Decision Trees	Creates a tree-like model for decision-making.	Product recommendation engines.
Support Vector Machines (SVMs)	Finds the best separation between categories.	Image classification on websites.
Neural Networks	Mimics the human brain for complex patterns.	AI-driven chatbots and NLP applications.

Example of Supervised Learning in Web Development

AI-Powered Search Engines
Search engines like **Google and Bing** use supervised learning to improve search

result rankings. By analyzing **past user queries and interactions**, AI models learn which search results are most relevant and **prioritize them** for future queries.

Chatbot Sentiment Analysis
Customer support chatbots use **supervised learning** to classify customer sentiments (e.g., happy, neutral, frustrated). This enables bots to **respond more appropriately** to user emotions, improving engagement and satisfaction.

---

2. Unsupervised Learning

Unsupervised learning deals with **unlabeled data**, meaning the model is not given predefined outputs. Instead, it explores data to **find hidden patterns, structures, or relationships** on its own.

This type of learning is particularly useful when dealing with **large datasets where human-labeled data is unavailable or impractical to obtain**.

How Unsupervised Learning Works

1. **Raw Data Input** – The model receives an **unstructured dataset** without labeled outputs.
2. **Pattern Detection** – The algorithm groups similar data points or identifies anomalies.
3. **Insights & Clustering** – The model organizes data into meaningful categories.
4. **Usage in Applications** – Developers use these insights for personalization, recommendations, or fraud detection.

Unsupervised Learning Algorithms

Algorithm	Description	Use Case in Web Development
K-Means Clustering	Groups data into clusters based on similarity.	Grouping website visitors by behavior.

Hierarchical Clustering	Creates a tree-based hierarchy of data groups.	Customer segmentation for targeted marketing.
Principal Component Analysis (PCA)	Reduces dimensionality while preserving key data.	Optimizing high-dimensional datasets in AI models.
Autoencoders	Compress and reconstruct data patterns.	Image enhancement for AI-driven photo editing tools.

Example of Unsupervised Learning in Web Development

E-Commerce Customer Segmentation
E-commerce websites use **unsupervised learning** to categorize customers based on shopping behavior. Instead of manually defining user groups, the AI model identifies customer segments like **frequent buyers, seasonal shoppers, and discount hunters**.

Anomaly Detection in Web Security
Unsupervised learning helps in **cybersecurity** by detecting **suspicious behavior patterns**. If a login attempt deviates from normal user behavior (e.g., logging in from a new country or making rapid transactions), the AI system **flags it as potential fraud**.

3. Reinforcement Learning

Reinforcement learning (RL) is an advanced form of ML where an **agent interacts with an environment** and learns through **trial and error** by receiving **rewards or penalties**.

Unlike supervised learning (which uses labeled data) or unsupervised learning (which finds patterns), reinforcement learning is designed to **learn dynamically from real-time interactions**.

How Reinforcement Learning Works

1. **Agent & Environment** – The AI agent operates in an environment (e.g., a website or a chatbot system).
2. **Actions & Feedback** – The agent takes actions and receives **positive or negative rewards** based on success.
3. **Policy Learning** – The model refines its strategy over time to **maximize rewards**.
4. **Continuous Improvement** – The agent improves through **self-learning** without human intervention.

Reinforcement Learning Algorithms

Algorithm	Description	Use Case in Web Development
Q-Learning	AI learns the best action for each state.	AI-powered web navigation assistants.
Deep Q-Networks (DQN)	Uses neural networks for complex decision-making.	AI-driven website optimization.
Policy Gradient Methods	Learns by improving action probabilities.	Automated UX design enhancements.

Example of Reinforcement Learning in Web Development

AI-Powered A/B Testing for UX Optimization
Reinforcement learning is used in **website A/B testing**, where AI continuously learns from **user interactions** and **automatically adjusts website layouts, colors, or button placements** to maximize conversions.

AI Chatbots That Learn From Conversations
Reinforcement learning allows **customer support chatbots** to **improve responses** by analyzing past conversations and refining future interactions based on what works best.

Understanding **supervised, unsupervised, and reinforcement learning** is crucial for developers integrating AI into web applications. Each ML type serves a unique function, from **predicting user behavior** to **improving security and automating web experiences**. The future of web development will continue to **leverage ML to enhance user engagement, security, and performance.**

Machine Learning in Web-Based Applications

Machine learning (ML) is transforming web applications by making them more **intelligent, adaptive, and user-centric**. Unlike traditional web applications, which rely on **predefined rules and static interactions**, ML-driven applications learn from **user data, interactions, and real-time feedback** to enhance performance and provide **personalized experiences**.

This section explores how machine learning is being implemented in **modern web-based applications**, optimizing user engagement, security, search capabilities, and automation.

1. Personalized User Experiences with ML

One of the most significant applications of ML in web development is **personalization**. Websites use ML algorithms to analyze **user preferences, behavior, and past interactions** to tailor content, recommendations, and experiences dynamically.

Key ML Techniques for Personalization

Technique	Description	Use Case
Collaborative Filtering	Recommends content based on similar user preferences.	Netflix suggesting movies based on watch history.

Content-Based Filtering	Recommends items based on a user's previous selections.	Amazon recommending similar products.
Deep Learning-Based Personalization	Uses neural networks to predict **future user behavior**.	YouTube's AI-driven video suggestions.

Example: AI-Powered Recommendation Systems

- **E-Commerce Websites (Amazon, eBay)** → Suggest products based on shopping history.
- **Streaming Platforms (Netflix, YouTube, Spotify)** → Recommend content based on user watch/listen habits.
- **News Aggregators (Google News, Apple News)** → Show articles based on past reading behavior.

Machine learning ensures that **each user receives a unique experience**, increasing engagement and retention rates.

---

2. AI-Powered Search and Auto-Suggestions

Traditional search engines rely on **keyword-based algorithms**, but ML-powered search engines understand **user intent**, **context**, and **natural language** to improve accuracy.

Key ML Features in Search Optimization

Feature	Description	Example

Semantic Search	Understands the meaning of words, not just exact matches.	Google's AI-powered search (BERT model).
Auto-Sug gestions	Predicts search queries before the user completes typing.	Google's autocomplete feature.
Visual Search	Allows users to search using images instead of text.	Pinterest's AI-driven visual search tool.

Example: AI-Powered Search Optimization

- **Google's RankBrain AI** analyzes **user behavior and search patterns** to deliver more relevant results.
- **E-commerce sites** like **eBay and Amazon** use ML to refine search results based on user history and preferences.
- **Pinterest and Instagram** allow users to **search for products using images**, powered by deep learning.

By leveraging ML in search, web applications can **improve accuracy, reduce bounce rates, and enhance user experience**.

---

3. AI-Powered Chatbots and Virtual Assistants

Chatbots powered by **machine learning and natural language processing (NLP)** have revolutionized **customer support, sales, and engagement** on websites.

How ML-Driven Chatbots Work

1. **NLP Understanding** – AI chatbots interpret user queries and analyze intent.
2. **Machine Learning Feedback Loop** – They improve responses based on past interactions.

3. **Conversational AI** – Advanced models like **GPT-4, Dialogflow, and IBM Watson** create human-like conversations.

Types of AI-Powered Chatbots

Type	Function	Example
Rule-Based Bots	Follow predefined responses.	Basic customer support bots.
Self-Learning Chatbots	Use ML to improve over time.	OpenAI GPT-powered bots.
Voice Assistants	Understand spoken commands.	Alexa, Google Assistant, Siri.

Example: AI Chatbots in Web Applications

- **E-Commerce** → AI-powered bots suggest products, answer FAQs, and assist in purchases (e.g., Shopify AI Chatbot).
- **Customer Support** → Chatbots reduce **response time and workload** (e.g., Intercom AI assistant).
- **Banking & Finance** → AI bots provide **account information and fraud alerts** (e.g., Bank of America's Erica AI).

By integrating **ML chatbots into web applications**, businesses **improve user engagement, reduce costs, and enhance customer satisfaction**.

---

4. Fraud Detection and Cybersecurity

Web applications are increasingly using ML to **detect fraud, prevent cyber threats, and enhance security**. Traditional security models rely on **predefined rules**, but ML-based systems **adapt dynamically** to detect **anomalies and malicious activities**.

How ML Enhances Web Security

ML Technique	Function	Example
Anomaly Detection	Identifies unusual activity based on patterns.	Detecting fraudulent credit card transactions.
Behavioral Analysis	Tracks user interactions for suspicious behavior.	AI-based CAPTCHA replacements.
Automated Threat Detection	Predicts potential cyberattacks before they occur.	Google's Safe Browsing AI.

Example: ML in Web Security

- **AI-based fraud detection** → PayPal uses ML to detect fraudulent transactions.
- **AI-powered CAPTCHA systems** → Google's **reCAPTCHA v3** identifies bots without requiring user interaction.
- **Predictive cybersecurity** → AI models predict **DDoS attacks and malware intrusions** before they happen.

By **automating cybersecurity with ML**, web applications can detect **threats in real-time**, ensuring better protection for users.

5. Automated Web Development and Design Optimization

Machine learning is **reducing manual effort** in web development by **automating design processes, optimizing user interfaces (UI), and enhancing user experience (UX)**.

ML-Powered Web Design Enhancements

Feature	Function	Example
AI-Generated Websites	Auto-designs sites based on user input.	Wix ADI (Artificial Design Intelligence).
Automated A/B Testing	Uses ML to test UI elements and improve conversions.	Google Optimize AI-driven testing.
Personalized UI/UX Adjustments	Dynamically adapts website layouts based on user behavior.	Netflix's AI-driven UI personalization.

Example: AI in Web Design

- **Adobe Sensei AI** → Enhances **image editing and layout optimization** for designers.
- **Figma AI Plugins** → Suggest **design improvements based on user trends**.
- **Wix AI Website Builder** → Auto-generates web pages with **minimal human input**.

AI is **automating** the creative and **decision-making process**, making web development faster and more **data-driven**.

6. Machine Learning in Web Performance Optimization

Web applications must **load quickly and perform efficiently** to retain users. Machine learning is improving website performance through **intelligent resource allocation, caching, and predictive optimizations**.

How ML Enhances Web Performance

Feature	Description	Example
AI-Based Image Compression	Reduces image file sizes without loss of quality.	Google's AI-powered WebP format.
Predictive Caching	Preloads content that a user is likely to visit next.	AI-powered CDN networks.
Adaptive Video Streaming	Adjusts video quality dynamically based on bandwidth.	YouTube's ML-based streaming optimizations.

Example: AI-Driven Performance Optimization

- **Google's PageSpeed AI** → Suggests **AI-based speed optimizations** for websites.
- **Cloudflare's AI CDN** → Uses ML to predict **server loads and optimize content delivery**.
- **AI-Driven Video Encoding** → Netflix optimizes video quality based on **device type and internet speed**.

Machine learning ensures that **web applications remain fast, efficient, and scalable** by dynamically adjusting **resources based on real-time demand**.

Real-World Use Cases of ML in Web Development

Industry	ML Application	Example
E-Commerce	Personalized product recommendations	Amazon, eBay
Streaming Services	AI-driven content suggestions	Netflix, Spotify
Customer Support	AI-powered chatbots	Intercom, Drift AI
Cybersecurity	Fraud detection	PayPal, Google reCAPTCHA
Search Engines	AI-enhanced search	Google RankBrain, Bing AI
Website Builders	Automated web design	Wix AI, Adobe Sensei

Machine learning is **reshaping** web development, making applications **more intelligent, responsive, and secure**. The future of web applications lies in **AI-driven automation, personalization, and predictive analytics**, ensuring better user experiences and business success.

Chapter 3

Key AI Technologies for Web Development

Natural Language Processing (NLP) for Web Applications

Introduction to NLP in Web Development

Natural Language Processing (NLP) is a branch of artificial intelligence (AI) that enables machines to understand, interpret, and respond to human language. It plays a crucial role in modern web applications by **enhancing user interactions, automating responses, and improving content comprehension**.

Web applications use NLP to power **chatbots, voice assistants, text analytics, sentiment analysis, and AI-driven search functionalities**. As users demand more intuitive and interactive web experiences, NLP is becoming an essential technology for **engagement, automation, and personalization**.

How NLP Works in Web Applications

NLP is built on a combination of **linguistics, machine learning, and deep learning models** that allow web applications to process and understand human language.

The fundamental process of NLP involves the following steps:

1. **Text Preprocessing**

   - Tokenization: Breaking text into words or phrases.
   - Lemmatization & Stemming: Converting words to their base forms (e.g., "running" → "run").
   - Stopword Removal: Filtering out common words like "the," "is," and "a" to focus on key terms.

2. **Feature Extraction**

   - Named Entity Recognition (NER): Identifying important entities such as names, dates, locations.
   - Part-of-Speech (POS) Tagging: Assigning grammatical categories to words (e.g., noun, verb).
   - Word Embeddings: Converting text into numerical vectors for machine learning models.

3. **Machine Learning & Deep Learning Models**

   - Recurrent Neural Networks (RNNs) and Transformers (e.g., BERT, GPT) analyze text for meaning and intent.
   - Pre-trained models improve accuracy in tasks such as text generation, translation, and question answering.

4. **Natural Language Understanding (NLU) & Natural Language Generation (NLG)**

   - NLU: Comprehends the meaning of the text.
   - NLG: Generates human-like responses based on context.

Applications of NLP in Web Development

1. AI-Powered Chatbots & Virtual Assistants

NLP is the foundation of **chatbots and AI-powered customer service assistants**, allowing them to understand and respond to user queries intelligently.

How NLP Enhances Chatbots:

- **Context Awareness:** AI-powered chatbots remember past conversations for better responses.
- **Multilingual Support:** NLP enables real-time translation and multilingual customer service.
- **Sentiment Analysis:** Bots detect user emotions and adjust responses accordingly.

Examples:

- **Google Dialogflow** – Creates AI chatbots for websites and apps.
- **IBM Watson Assistant** – Enhances customer interactions with AI-driven conversations.

- **OpenAI GPT Models** – Power conversational AI chatbots for real-time web interactions.

---

2. AI-Powered Search and Auto-Suggestions

NLP improves **search engines on websites**, making them more **context-aware and intuitive**.

How NLP Improves Search:

- **Semantic Search:** Understands **user intent** rather than relying on exact keyword matching.
- **Auto-Suggestions:** Predicts search queries in real-time as users type.
- **Voice Search Integration:** Converts speech to text and processes user requests.

Examples:

- **Google's BERT Model** – Enhances search ranking by understanding sentence structure.
- **E-Commerce AI Search (Amazon, eBay)** – Delivers personalized search results based on user behavior.

---

3. Sentiment Analysis & Opinion Mining

Web applications use NLP to analyze **user feedback, product reviews, and social media comments** to determine public sentiment.

How Sentiment Analysis Works:

- **Positive, Negative, Neutral Classification:** Determines the emotional tone of a statement.
- **Brand Reputation Monitoring:** Detects potential PR issues from customer feedback.
- **Content Moderation:** Identifies and removes inappropriate language from forums and social platforms.

Examples:

- **Twitter's AI Sentiment Analysis** – Monitors trending topics and user emotions.
- **Amazon Reviews Analysis** – Summarizes customer feedback using AI.

---

4. AI-Based Content Generation & Translation

Web applications use NLP to **automate content creation and translation**, making content more accessible.

Key NLP Features for Content Management:

- **AI Text Generation:** Automates blog writing, captions, and summaries.
- **Real-Time Language Translation:** Converts text between languages for global reach.
- **Grammar & Spelling Corrections:** AI-powered tools assist with writing enhancement.

Examples:

- **Google Translate** – Uses deep learning to enhance translation accuracy.
- **Grammarly AI Editor** – Provides grammar and style improvements in writing.

NLP Tools and APIs for Web Applications

Tool	Description	Use Case
Google Cloud NLP	Sentiment analysis, text classification.	AI-based customer feedback monitoring.
IBM Watson NLP	AI-powered chatbot development.	Enhancing e-commerce support.
OpenAI GPT API	AI-driven text generation.	Chatbots, AI content creation.
Amazon Comprehend	Entity recognition, language detection.	AI-driven search and analytics.

With **NLP-powered AI**, websites are becoming **more interactive, intelligent, and adaptive**, significantly improving **user engagement and automation**.

Computer Vision and Image Recognition on Websites

Introduction to Computer Vision in Web Applications

Computer vision is an AI technology that enables web applications to **process, analyze, and interpret visual data** from images and videos. This field is widely used for **image recognition, facial authentication, object detection, and automated content moderation**.

With the rise of **e-commerce, social media, and security-driven web applications**, computer vision is now a key AI component in **enhancing visual interactions on websites**.

How Computer Vision Works

1. **Image Acquisition** – Capturing images through a camera or uploading visual data.
2. **Preprocessing** – Enhancing images (removing noise, adjusting brightness, resizing).
3. **Feature Extraction** – Detecting edges, colors, textures, and objects.
4. **Deep Learning Models** – Neural networks (CNNs) analyze patterns to recognize objects.
5. **Decision Making** – AI interprets the image and performs tasks (e.g., facial recognition, object detection).

Applications of Computer Vision in Web Development

1. AI-Powered Image Search & Recognition

Web applications leverage **computer vision** to enable **image-based search functionality**.

Examples:

- **Google Lens** – Allows users to search for products using photos instead of text.
- **Pinterest Visual Search** – Identifies objects in images to suggest related content.
- **E-Commerce Platforms (Amazon, Alibaba)** – Users search for similar products by uploading images.

---

2. Facial Recognition for Authentication

Many web applications integrate **AI-powered facial recognition** for security, personalization, and authentication.

Examples:

- **Apple Face ID & Google Photos AI** – Organizes photos based on facial recognition.
- **Banking & Finance Websites** – Use face verification for login security.
- **Retail & E-Commerce** – AI-based virtual try-on features for fashion and makeup brands.

---

3. Automated Content Moderation & Image Filtering

Web applications use **computer vision** to detect **inappropriate or sensitive content** in images uploaded by users.

Examples:

- **Facebook AI Moderation** – Detects and removes explicit images.
- **YouTube AI Filtering** – Scans and flags inappropriate content in videos.
- **Online Marketplaces (eBay, Craigslist)** – Automatically filters product images that violate guidelines.

---

4. AI-Powered Augmented Reality (AR) for Web Applications

Computer vision is widely used in **augmented reality (AR) experiences**, allowing users to interact with digital objects.

33

Examples:

- **IKEA Place App** – Uses AR to visualize furniture in real-world spaces.
- **Snapchat & Instagram Filters** – Apply AI-based visual effects in real time.
- **Virtual Dressing Rooms (Zara, Sephora)** – Allows customers to try on clothing or makeup virtually.

Computer Vision Tools & APIs for Web Applications

Tool	Description	Use Case
Google Vision AI	Detects objects, faces, and text in images.	AI-powered search & security.
Amazon Rekognition	Image & video analysis.	Facial authentication & moderation.
OpenCV	Open-source computer vision library.	Image enhancement & object detection.
Microsoft Azure Computer Vision	Optical character recognition (OCR).	AI-powered document scanning.

By integrating **computer vision into web applications**, businesses **enhance user experiences, security, and interactivity**, making AI-driven websites **more dynamic and visually intelligent**.

Deep Learning and Neural Networks in Web-Based AI

Introduction to Deep Learning in Web Applications

Deep learning is a **subset of machine learning (ML)** that uses artificial neural networks (ANNs) to **process complex data, recognize patterns, and make intelligent decisions**. Unlike traditional ML models, deep learning can **handle unstructured data such as images, audio, and text**, making it ideal for

AI-powered web applications that require **advanced automation and intelligence**.

Neural networks enable web applications to **personalize user experiences, improve recommendations, enhance security, and automate interactions**. Many modern web technologies, including **chatbots, search engines, recommendation systems, and content analysis tools**, use deep learning to provide **real-time and data-driven functionalities**.

Understanding Neural Networks for Web-Based AI

Artificial Neural Networks (ANNs) mimic the **human brain's structure** by processing information through layers of neurons. Each layer **extracts features** from the input data, refines them, and passes them forward to produce an **accurate output**.

Structure of a Neural Network

1. **Input Layer** → Receives raw data (e.g., images, text, user behavior).
2. **Hidden Layers** → Processes data using neurons and applies weights to extract patterns.
3. **Output Layer** → Produces final predictions or decisions.

Types of Neural Networks Used in Web Applications

Neural Network Type	Function	Web Application Example
Convolutional Neural Networks (CNNs)	Image recognition and classification	AI-powered product search, facial recognition
Recurrent Neural Networks (RNNs)	Text processing, speech recognition	AI chatbots, language translation
Transformers (BERT, GPT)	Context-aware text understanding	AI content generation, AI-powered search

Autoencoders	Dimensionality reduction, anomaly detection	AI-driven data compression, fraud detection

Applications of Deep Learning in Web Development

1. AI-Powered Content Generation

Deep learning enables **AI-driven text, image, and video generation**, revolutionizing web-based content creation.

Examples:

- **OpenAI GPT-4** generates human-like text for blogs, chatbots, and customer support.
- **DeepAI and Runway ML** create AI-generated visuals for websites.
- **Synthesia** uses deep learning to generate AI-powered video content.

2. AI-Based Web Search Optimization

Deep learning enhances search engines by **understanding context, intent, and relevance** rather than relying on basic keyword matching.

Examples:

- **Google's BERT (Bidirectional Encoder Representations from Transformers)** improves search accuracy by interpreting **natural language queries**.
- **E-commerce websites (Amazon, eBay)** use AI to deliver **more relevant search results** based on past user behavior.

3. AI-Driven Image and Video Analysis

Neural networks help websites **automate image recognition, content filtering, and visual search functionalities**.

Examples:

- **Pinterest AI** enables users to search products using **image-based searches**.
- **YouTube AI** automates **video recommendations** based on deep learning models.

---

4. AI-Based Fraud Detection & Security

Deep learning models **identify patterns and detect anomalies**, enhancing web security and fraud detection.

Examples:

- **PayPal AI Fraud Detection** uses deep learning to analyze millions of transactions for **fraudulent activities**.
- **Google reCAPTCHA AI** differentiates human users from bots using deep learning techniques.

Benefits of Deep Learning for Web Development

- **Higher Accuracy:** Learns from data over time to **refine and improve performance**.
- **Scalability:** Handles **large-scale web applications** with vast amounts of data.
- **Automation:** Reduces **manual intervention** in content moderation, recommendations, and security.

Deep learning is **at the core of AI-driven web development**, enabling **personalized, efficient, and highly interactive user experiences**.

Reinforcement Learning for Personalized User Experience

What is Reinforcement Learning?

Reinforcement Learning (RL) is a machine learning technique where an **AI agent learns through trial and error** by interacting with an environment. The AI **receives**

rewards for correct actions and penalties for incorrect ones, gradually optimizing its performance.

Unlike **supervised learning**, where models learn from labeled data, RL **learns dynamically** by making decisions and **adapting in real-time**.

How Reinforcement Learning Works in Web Applications

1. **Agent** – The AI-powered system that makes decisions (e.g., recommendation engine).
2. **Environment** – The digital space where the AI interacts (e.g., an e-commerce website).
3. **Actions** – Choices made by the AI (e.g., suggesting a product).
4. **Rewards & Penalties** – AI gets rewarded for correct actions and penalized for incorrect ones.
5. **Learning Policy** – The model adjusts its behavior based on past outcomes.

Reinforcement Learning in Web Development

1. AI-Powered Personalization Engines

Reinforcement learning optimizes **user experiences by adapting to individual preferences over time**.

Examples:

- **Netflix's Recommendation AI** improves **movie suggestions** as users interact with the platform.
- **Spotify AI** personalizes playlists based on **listening history and feedback**.

---

2. AI-Driven A/B Testing & UX Optimization

Reinforcement learning automates **A/B testing**, improving website layouts, color schemes, and call-to-action placements.

Examples:

- **Google Optimize AI** dynamically tests different **website designs** to enhance conversions.
- **E-commerce websites** adjust pricing and discounts using RL-based **real-time analytics**.

---

3. AI-Powered Chatbots with Adaptive Learning

Chatbots that use **reinforcement learning** improve their **response accuracy over time** by learning from **real-world conversations**.

Examples:

- **Customer support bots (Intercom, Drift AI)** refine answers based on **past user interactions**.
- **AI-driven language tutors** adjust difficulty levels based on user progress.

Reinforcement learning **enables dynamic, self-improving AI systems**, enhancing **personalized user engagement**.

AI APIs and Libraries: TensorFlow.js, OpenAI, IBM Watson, Google AI

1. TensorFlow.js: AI-Powered Web Machine Learning

TensorFlow.js is a **JavaScript-based machine learning library** that allows AI models to run directly in web browsers.

Features:

- Runs AI models **without a backend server**.
- Enables **real-time AI applications** on the web.
- Supports **image recognition, text classification, and neural networks**.

Use Cases:

- **AI-Powered Image Processing** – Real-time face detection in **web-based video applications**.
- **Interactive AI Chatbots** – Running **AI-driven NLP models** in browsers without backend dependency.

2. OpenAI API: AI-Powered Text and Image Generation

The **OpenAI API** provides **natural language processing (NLP) and image generation** capabilities using deep learning.

Features:

- **GPT-4 AI for text generation, chatbots, and content automation**.
- **DALL·E AI for AI-generated images and visual enhancements**.

Use Cases:

- **AI-Generated Blogs & Summaries** – Automating content creation in news websites.
- **AI-Powered Customer Support** – Advanced NLP-driven chatbots.

3. IBM Watson AI API: AI for Web Applications

IBM Watson provides **pre-trained AI models** for NLP, voice recognition, and AI-powered decision-making.

Features:

- **AI Speech Recognition & Language Understanding**.
- **Machine Learning-Powered Data Insights**.

Use Cases:

- **Voice Assistants** – AI-powered **speech-to-text and text-to-speech** conversions.
- **AI-Driven Business Analytics** – Automated **decision-making in finance and healthcare web apps**.

4. Google AI API: AI-Powered Web Intelligence

Google AI provides **a suite of machine learning APIs** for **vision, NLP, translation, and speech recognition**.

Features:

- **Google Vision API** – Recognizes objects, faces, and text in images.
- **Google Translate AI** – Provides AI-powered multilingual support.

Use Cases:

- **E-Commerce AI Product Recognition** – Identifying **products from user-uploaded images**.
- **AI-Based Content Moderation** – Detecting **inappropriate web content automatically**.

AI-powered APIs and libraries like **TensorFlow.js, OpenAI, IBM Watson, and Google AI** are **accelerating AI integration in web applications**, enabling **faster, smarter, and more interactive digital experiences**.

41

Chapter 4

Enhancing User Experience with AI

AI-Powered UI/UX Optimization

Introduction to AI in UI/UX Design

User Interface (UI) and User Experience (UX) design are crucial components of any web application. A well-designed UI ensures an intuitive, visually appealing interface, while UX focuses on **seamless interaction, usability, and user satisfaction**. Traditionally, UI/UX designers relied on **manual research, user testing, and static design principles** to optimize web applications. However, with advancements in **artificial intelligence (AI)**, UI/UX design is undergoing a significant transformation.

AI-powered tools analyze **user behavior, automate design adjustments, and personalize interfaces in real-time**. Websites and applications are now capable of dynamically optimizing layouts, fonts, colors, and content to enhance user engagement and **reduce friction in user interactions**.

How AI is Revolutionizing UI/UX Optimization

Artificial intelligence in UI/UX design leverages **machine learning, deep learning, and predictive analytics** to improve the **visual appeal, usability, and accessibility** of web applications. AI-driven UI/UX optimization involves:

1. **Automating User Research and Behavior Analysis**

   - AI analyzes **user heatmaps, scroll behavior, and click interactions** to identify design flaws.
   - Data-driven insights replace **traditional manual surveys** and subjective design choices.
2. **Personalized Web Interfaces**

   - AI customizes UI elements like **buttons, navigation, and color schemes** based on user preferences.

- Web applications adapt to individual **browsing patterns and accessibility needs**.
3. **Dynamic Layout Adjustments**

   - AI-driven layouts optimize page structures based on **real-time user interaction data**.
   - Websites change dynamically to suit different devices, screen sizes, and user personas.
4. **Real-Time Feedback and Design Improvements**

   - AI analyzes **real-time interactions** to detect frustration points and suggests design modifications.
   - AI-generated UI recommendations streamline **workflow for designers and developers**.

Key AI Technologies Used in UI/UX Optimization

AI Technology	Function in UI/UX Design	Example
Machine Learning (ML)	Analyzes user interactions, predicts behavior	Amazon's AI-driven layout optimization
Neural Networks (NNs)	Automates complex UI adjustments based on past interactions	Adobe Sensei AI-powered design enhancements
Computer Vision	Recognizes visual patterns for accessibility adjustments	AI-driven image scaling for responsive web design
Natural Language	Improves chatbot-driven	AI-powered voice search and assistant UI in e-commerce

Processing (NLP)	navigation and interaction	

AI-Powered UI Personalization

1. Adaptive UI Based on User Preferences

Web applications powered by AI can adapt UI elements dynamically for **different users, devices, and demographics**.

Examples:

- **E-Commerce:** Websites adjust **font sizes, layouts, and navigation menus** based on user behavior.
- **Streaming Services:** Platforms like **Netflix** personalize interface layouts for different users.
- **Corporate Websites:** AI-driven dashboards change UI components based on **employee roles** and workflow needs.

2. AI-Based Color and Font Optimization

AI-driven UI tools **select colors and fonts** that improve readability, accessibility, and engagement.

Examples:

- **Canva AI Suggestion Engine** helps designers choose **optimal color palettes**.
- **AI-Generated Contrast Adjustments** improve visibility for visually impaired users.

AI in UX Optimization for Seamless Navigation

1. AI-Powered Voice and Chat-Based Navigation

Voice-controlled UI and AI-powered chatbots **enhance website navigation** by making interactions more natural and hands-free.

- **Google Assistant and Siri Web Navigation** – Users can browse the web through voice commands.
- **AI Chatbots for Search Assistance** – Chatbots guide users to **relevant pages, products, or services**.

2. AI-Driven Predictive User Actions

AI predicts **user intentions** based on historical behavior and **auto-suggests navigation paths**.

Examples:

- **Amazon's AI-Powered Navigation** anticipates what users want to buy next.
- **Google's Predictive Search AI** refines auto-suggestions based on past queries.

Benefits of AI-Powered UI/UX Optimization

Benefit	Description	Example
Higher User Engagement	AI tailors UI based on user habits	Spotify AI-curated music playlists
Reduced Bounce Rates	Intelligent UI layouts improve usability	AI-based content recommendation engines
Enhanced Accessibility	AI adjusts UI for users with disabilities	AI-powered screen readers for visually impaired users
Real-Time Adaptability	Interfaces evolve based on user feedback	E-commerce AI adjusting product display based on browsing history

AI-driven UI/UX optimization is transforming web design, enabling businesses to **deliver highly personalized, accessible, and efficient user experiences**.

Intelligent A/B Testing for Better Designs

Introduction to AI-Powered A/B Testing

A/B testing, also known as **split testing**, is a process where two versions of a web page, UI design, or feature are tested to determine **which one performs better**. Traditionally, A/B testing requires **manual setup, user segmentation, and long testing cycles**.

AI-powered A/B testing introduces **automation, predictive analytics, and dynamic optimization**, ensuring **real-time design improvements** with minimal human intervention.

How AI Enhances A/B Testing

1. **Automated Experimentation**

   - AI **generates multiple test variations automatically**.
   - Eliminates the need for **manual test configuration**.

2. **Real-Time Data Collection and Analysis**

   - AI **analyzes user interactions continuously**, adapting tests dynamically.
   - Provides **instant feedback** instead of waiting weeks for results.

3. **Predictive Performance Insights**

   - AI uses **historical data and deep learning models** to predict **which design will perform best**.

4. **Adaptive Optimization**

   - AI adjusts **website UI elements** in real time, improving performance without **waiting for A/B test completion**.

Key AI Algorithms Used in A/B Testing

AI Algorithm	Function in A/B Testing	Example
Multi-Armed Bandit (MAB)	Dynamically shifts traffic to best-performing design variant	Google Ads AI-based ad placement optimization
Bayesian Optimization	Predicts best test variations using probability models	AI-driven UI optimization in SaaS applications
Reinforcement Learning (RL)	AI self-learns from test data to continuously improve	Netflix AI-based UX personalization

AI-Powered A/B Testing Tools

Tool	Function	Example
Google Optimize AI	Automated A/B testing for website layouts	AI-driven UI testing for e-commerce
Adobe Target AI	Predictive AI testing for personalized experiences	Real-time content recommendations
VWO AI Testing	AI-powered UX testing and analytics	AI-enhanced customer experience insights

Examples of AI-Driven A/B Testing in Web Development

1. AI-Powered Website UI Optimization

Companies use AI to **test different navigation layouts, color schemes, and button placements**.

Example:

- **Booking.com AI A/B Testing** – AI tests multiple homepage designs and dynamically selects the most engaging version.

2. AI-Based E-Commerce Product Display Optimization

AI tests different **product placements, discount banners, and shopping cart layouts** to increase conversions.

Example:

- **Amazon AI-Powered Product Page Testing** – AI adjusts product descriptions and images based on user engagement.

3. AI-Driven Content Personalization

AI **optimizes blog headlines, article formats, and featured images** for higher engagement.

Example:

- **Medium AI-Powered Blog Testing** – AI determines which article styles generate more reader retention.

Benefits of AI-Enhanced A/B Testing

Benefit	Description	Example
Faster Testing Cycles	AI reduces testing time from weeks to hours	AI-automated UX testing in mobile apps

Higher Conversion Rates	AI dynamically selects best-performing variations	AI-driven call-to-action testing
Reduced Human Effort	AI automates data analysis and result interpretation	E-commerce AI optimizing checkout flows

AI-powered A/B testing enables businesses to **refine web experiences dynamically**, ensuring optimal **user engagement, satisfaction, and conversions**.

AI-Driven Personalization: How Netflix and Amazon Do It

Introduction to AI-Powered Personalization

Personalization in web applications has evolved from **static user preferences** to **real-time AI-driven experiences**. Companies like **Netflix and Amazon** leverage artificial intelligence (AI) to analyze user behavior, predict interests, and deliver **hyper-personalized content, product recommendations, and dynamic UI adjustments**.

Traditional personalization relied on **predefined rules**, whereas AI-powered personalization continuously **learns, adapts, and evolves** based on user interactions. This approach **increases engagement, retention, and conversions** by ensuring users see content or products most relevant to them.

How Netflix Uses AI for Personalization

Netflix is a **data-driven streaming platform** that uses AI and machine learning to provide users with **highly personalized content recommendations, dynamic thumbnails, and adaptive user interfaces**.

1. AI-Powered Content Recommendation System

Netflix employs a **hybrid AI recommendation system** that combines:

- **Collaborative Filtering** → Suggests content based on similar user preferences.
- **Content-Based Filtering** → Recommends shows similar to what a user has watched.
- **Deep Learning & Reinforcement Learning** → Learns from **watch patterns, ratings, viewing time, and interactions** to refine recommendations.

Example:

- If a user watches multiple **crime dramas**, Netflix's AI will recommend similar content, even if the user has never searched for it.

2. AI-Generated Thumbnails for User Engagement

Netflix personalizes not only what content is recommended but **how it is presented**.

- AI dynamically selects the **best thumbnail images** based on a user's viewing history.
- Different users see **different thumbnails** for the same show, increasing the likelihood of engagement.

Example:

- A user who watches more **romantic movies** will see a thumbnail featuring a **romantic scene**, while an **action movie fan** will see a more **intense action-focused** thumbnail.

3. AI-Optimized Streaming Quality

Netflix uses AI-powered algorithms to:

- **Adjust video quality based on internet speed** (adaptive bitrate streaming).
- **Optimize server load balancing** for a seamless experience.

By continuously learning from user interactions, Netflix ensures that every viewer gets a **customized, engaging, and seamless streaming experience**.

How Amazon Uses AI for Personalization

Amazon is one of the pioneers of **AI-driven e-commerce personalization**, leveraging **machine learning, predictive analytics, and deep learning** to optimize shopping experiences.

1. AI-Powered Product Recommendations

Amazon's recommendation engine accounts for:

- **User Browsing History** → Predicts future purchases based on past activity.
- **Purchase Behavior** → Suggests complementary products.
- **Trending Data** → Displays products based on global shopping trends.

Example:

- If a user searches for **laptops**, Amazon's AI will recommend related accessories like **laptop bags, cooling pads, and external drives**.

2. AI-Powered Dynamic Pricing & Discounts

Amazon adjusts prices in real-time using AI-driven **dynamic pricing models**.

- AI analyzes **demand, competitor pricing, and purchase history** to suggest optimal prices.
- Customers may receive **personalized discounts** based on their purchase patterns.

3. AI-Powered Search and Voice Shopping

Amazon's AI enhances search functionality by:

- **Predicting search queries** before users finish typing.
- **Using NLP-powered voice search** (via Alexa) to help users find products through speech.

Example:

- If a user searches for "wireless headphones," Amazon's AI might suggest **highly rated products based on user preferences**.

The Impact of AI-Driven Personalization in Web Applications

Feature	Netflix Implementation	Amazon Implementation
Recommendation System	Suggests movies based on watch history.	Suggests products based on purchase behavior.
Dynamic UI	Custom thumbnails and UI adjustments.	AI-based product placement and categorization.
AI-Optimized Content	Predicts trending movies and shows.	Predicts best-selling products.
AI-Driven Search	Auto-suggests relevant movies/shows.	Auto-completes and refines product searches.
Real-Time AI Analytics	Adjusts recommendations based on recent activity.	Optimizes pricing based on demand.

Both companies **leverage AI-driven personalization** to **enhance user experience, drive engagement, and maximize revenue**.

Automated Dark Mode, Layout Adjustments, and Content Adaptation

Introduction to AI in Adaptive UI Design

Web applications today require **dynamic and personalized UI/UX adjustments** to cater to **different user preferences, devices, and environmental conditions**. AI-driven automation ensures that users get an **optimal viewing experience** with **adaptive themes, responsive layouts, and real-time content customization**.

AI-powered UI/UX adaptation focuses on:

- **Dark Mode & Theme Adjustments**
- **Layout Restructuring for Different Devices**
- **Content Adaptation Based on Context & User Behavior**

---

1. AI-Powered Dark Mode & Theme Adjustments

How AI Automates Dark Mode

Dark mode is a **popular UI trend** that reduces eye strain, saves battery life, and enhances readability in low-light conditions. AI can **automatically enable or adjust dark mode** based on:

- **User Preferences** → Detects if the user has enabled dark mode in system settings.
- **Ambient Light Detection** → AI adjusts the UI theme based on room brightness.
- **Usage Behavior** → AI learns when users prefer dark mode (e.g., evening hours) and automatically switches themes.

Examples of AI-Powered Dark Mode Implementations:

- **Google Chrome** → Detects system-wide dark mode settings and applies it to web pages.
- **iOS & Android Apps** → Use AI to **adjust themes dynamically** based on screen time.

53

2. AI-Driven Layout Adjustments for Responsive Web Design

How AI Optimizes Website Layouts Dynamically

Traditional responsive web design **relies on predefined media queries** for different screen sizes. AI takes this a step further by:

- **Analyzing user behavior** to predict the most effective layout.
- **Rearranging UI elements dynamically** based on screen size and device type.
- **Testing multiple layout versions** to select the one that maximizes engagement.

Examples of AI-Driven Layout Adaptation:

- **Amazon's AI-based grid system** → Dynamically adjusts product display based on device type.
- **Google's AI-powered adaptive UI** → Reconfigures search results layout for different screen sizes.

Benefits of AI-Driven Layout Adjustments

Feature	Benefit	Example
Device-Based Optimization	Adapts UI for smartphones, tablets, and desktops	AI-driven e-commerce layouts
Behavior-Based Layout Restructuring	Prioritizes high-engagement sections	Netflix UI personalization
Dynamic Grid Systems	AI adjusts grid layouts based on user interactions	Google search results formatting

3. AI-Powered Content Adaptation Based on Context

AI enhances **content presentation** by adapting it **based on user behavior, environment, and interaction patterns.**

How AI Automates Content Adaptation

- **Adaptive News Feeds** → AI tailors news articles based on reading habits.
- **Context-Aware UI Adjustments** → AI modifies **text size, spacing, and contrast** for accessibility.
- **Real-Time Content Optimization** → AI dynamically prioritizes **popular or trending content.**

Examples of AI-Powered Content Adaptation

Industry	AI Implementation	Example
News & Media	AI recommends news articles based on reading history.	Google News AI Feed
E-Commerce	AI highlights relevant product deals dynamically.	Amazon AI-Powered Discounts
Streaming Services	AI curates content based on mood and time of day.	Spotify AI Playlist Adaptation

AI-driven UI/UX adaptation is **redefining personalization in web applications,** ensuring **users get a seamless, responsive, and visually optimized experience.** AI-powered dark mode, adaptive layouts, and content customization create a **dynamic and personalized user journey,** improving engagement and satisfaction.

With companies like **Netflix, Amazon, Google, and Spotify leading the way,** AI-driven personalization is setting the **new standard for web design and interactivity.** The future of web applications will be **entirely AI-driven,** adapting in **real-time** to user needs, behaviors, and contexts.

Chapter 5

AI-Powered Chatbots and Virtual Assistants

Understanding AI Chatbots for Websites

Introduction to AI Chatbots

AI-powered chatbots are transforming web-based interactions by automating **customer support, user engagement, and business processes**. Unlike traditional rule-based chatbots that rely on **predefined scripts**, AI chatbots **understand natural language, learn from interactions, and respond dynamically to user queries**.

How AI Chatbots Work

An AI chatbot **simulates human conversation** by leveraging **Natural Language Processing (NLP), Machine Learning (ML), and Deep Learning**. Here's how an AI chatbot functions:

1. **User Input Processing** – The chatbot receives a query in **text or voice format**.
2. **Natural Language Understanding (NLU)** – AI analyzes the query, identifies **intent and context**, and extracts important keywords.
3. **Machine Learning Model Processing** – The AI engine **compares user input with stored data and past interactions** to determine the best response.
4. **Natural Language Generation (NLG)** – The chatbot **constructs a human-like response** and delivers it to the user.
5. **Continuous Learning** – The chatbot improves its responses over time using **machine learning algorithms**.

Types of AI Chatbots

Chatbot Type	Function	Example
Rule-Based Chatbots	Follows predefined scripts and fixed responses.	Simple FAQ bots.
AI-Powered Chatbots	Uses NLP and ML to understand and generate dynamic responses.	Customer support chatbots on e-commerce sites.
Hybrid Chatbots	Combines rule-based and AI-powered features.	Virtual assistants for businesses.
Voice Assistants	Processes voice commands and speaks responses.	Siri, Google Assistant, Alexa.

Benefits of AI Chatbots for Websites

1. 24/7 Customer Support

- AI chatbots **reduce response times** by providing instant answers, even outside business hours.
- Chatbots handle **multiple users simultaneously**, reducing the burden on human support agents.

2. Personalized User Interactions

- AI-powered chatbots **analyze user behavior, preferences, and past interactions** to offer **customized responses**.
- **E-commerce chatbots** suggest **personalized product recommendations** based on browsing history.

3. Cost Reduction & Increased Efficiency

- AI chatbots **replace traditional customer support agents**, reducing operational costs.
- Businesses automate **appointment bookings, order tracking, and FAQs** without human intervention.

4. Multilingual Support & Voice Assistance

- AI chatbots support **multiple languages**, enhancing user accessibility across different regions.
- Voice-enabled chatbots allow users to **speak instead of type**, making interactions more natural.

5. Data Collection & Business Insights

- Chatbots **track user interactions** and generate data for **customer insights, business intelligence, and trend analysis**.

Real-World Applications of AI Chatbots

Industry	Chatbot Use Case	Example
E-Commerce	AI-powered customer support, order tracking, and product recommendations.	Amazon's Alexa Shopping Bot
Banking & Finance	AI-driven fraud detection, customer queries, and loan processing.	Bank of America's Erica AI
Healthcare	Virtual assistants for medical advice, appointment booking, and symptom checking.	Babylon AI Health Bot

Education	AI tutors that assist students with learning concepts and FAQs.	Google's Socratic AI Tutor
Travel & Hospitality	AI chatbots for booking assistance, travel recommendations, and hotel reservations.	Expedia AI Travel Assistant

Using Dialogflow, OpenAI, and IBM Watson for Chatbot Development

Developers and businesses use various **AI platforms** to build chatbots that provide **intelligent and context-aware conversations**. Below are three major AI-powered chatbot development platforms:

1. Google Dialogflow: NLP-Based Chatbot Development

What is Dialogflow?

Google Dialogflow is an AI-powered **natural language understanding (NLU) platform** that allows developers to create **chatbots, voice assistants, and conversational agents** for websites, apps, and smart devices.

Key Features of Dialogflow

- **Pre-Built NLP Models** – Recognizes **intents, entities, and context** to process natural language queries.
- **Multichannel Deployment** – Integrates with **websites, Google Assistant, WhatsApp, Facebook Messenger, Slack, and more**.
- **Context Management** – Maintains **context-aware conversations** by remembering previous interactions.
- **Machine Learning-Based Training** – Continuously improves response accuracy by **learning from new data**.

Use Cases of Dialogflow in Web Applications

- **Customer Service Automation** – AI chatbots handle FAQs, refunds, and customer queries.

- **Voice-Enabled Virtual Assistants** – Power **AI voice search and smart assistants**.
- **Healthcare AI Assistants** – Provide **medical information and appointment scheduling**.

Example: Building a Chatbot with Dialogflow

1. **Create a Dialogflow Agent** – Define a chatbot's **personality and responses**.
2. **Train the Bot with Intents & Entities** – Input sample user queries to improve AI learning.
3. **Integrate with Web Applications** – Deploy the chatbot on **websites, mobile apps, or messaging platforms**.

---

2. OpenAI GPT-4: Advanced AI Chatbot Development

What is OpenAI GPT-4?

OpenAI's **GPT-4 (Generative Pre-trained Transformer 4)** is an **advanced NLP model** that generates **human-like responses** for chatbots and virtual assistants.

Key Features of GPT-4 for Chatbots

- **Conversational AI & Context Awareness** – Understands **complex queries, follows up, and adapts conversations dynamically**.
- **Text Generation & Personalization** – Generates **engaging, intelligent, and detailed responses**.
- **Multimodal Capabilities** – Supports **both text and image-based interactions**.
- **API Integration for Web Development** – Developers can integrate GPT-4 using **OpenAI API** for web-based AI chatbots.

Use Cases of GPT-4 in Chatbots

- **AI Customer Support Bots** – Automate **support tickets, troubleshooting, and live chat responses**.
- **AI Content Assistants** – Generate **email replies, blog suggestions, and social media posts**.
- **AI Sales Chatbots** – Help businesses **convert website visitors into customers**.

Example: Developing a GPT-4 Chatbot for Websites

1. **Access OpenAI's GPT-4 API** – Get an API key from **OpenAI's developer portal**.
2. **Train the Chatbot with Custom Prompts** – Fine-tune responses based on **business needs**.
3. **Integrate with Web Applications** – Deploy GPT-4-powered bots in **web apps, SaaS platforms, and CRM tools**.

---

3. IBM Watson: Enterprise-Grade AI Chatbot Development

What is IBM Watson Assistant?

IBM Watson Assistant is an **AI-powered conversational chatbot platform** that enables businesses to build **scalable, enterprise-grade virtual assistants**.

Key Features of IBM Watson Chatbots

- **AI-Powered Sentiment Analysis** – Detects user emotions and responds accordingly.
- **Omnichannel Integration** – Works across **websites, mobile apps, and customer support platforms**.
- **AI-Driven Decision Making** – Uses ML to **refine conversations over time**.
- **Enterprise Security & Compliance** – Ensures **high-level data protection** for financial and healthcare chatbots.

Use Cases of IBM Watson Chatbots

- **Banking AI Assistants** – Handle **account inquiries, fraud alerts, and financial advice**.
- **E-Commerce Virtual Assistants** – Guide users to **products, track orders, and provide support**.
- **Healthcare AI Chatbots** – Offer **patient assistance, medical diagnostics, and health monitoring**.

Example: Deploying a Watson Chatbot for Web Applications

1. **Set Up IBM Watson Assistant** – Define chatbot interactions and user flows.
2. **Train Watson with NLP Models** – Improve AI understanding through **machine learning training**.
3. **Deploy on a Website** – Integrate IBM Watson into **customer service portals and chat applications**.

AI-powered chatbots built with **Google Dialogflow, OpenAI GPT-4, and IBM Watson** provide **seamless, intelligent, and highly interactive experiences** for websites. Businesses across **e-commerce, healthcare, finance, and customer support** use AI chatbots to **enhance engagement, automate responses, and improve user satisfaction**.

Implementing AI Chatbots in JavaScript and Python

AI chatbots can be implemented in **JavaScript and Python**, two of the most popular languages for web development and AI-powered automation. JavaScript is widely used for front-end and back-end web applications, while Python is a leading language for **machine learning, natural language processing (NLP), and AI model development**.

In this section, we explore **how to develop AI chatbots using JavaScript and Python**, leveraging popular libraries and frameworks.

Building an AI Chatbot in JavaScript

JavaScript enables **real-time chatbot interactions** on websites, making it an excellent choice for **client-side chatbot applications**. Developers commonly use **Node.js** for back-end processing and APIs like **Dialogflow, OpenAI GPT-4, or IBM Watson** for AI-driven responses.

1. Setting Up a JavaScript Chatbot with Node.js

Step 1: Install Required Libraries

To build an AI chatbot using Node.js, install **Express.js** for the back-end and integrate an AI API like OpenAI's GPT-4.

bash

CopyEdit

```
npm init -y

npm install express body-parser axios dotenv
```

Step 2: Create a Node.js Server

Create a simple Express.js server to handle chatbot requests.

javascript

CopyEdit

```javascript
const express = require("express");
const bodyParser = require("body-parser");
const axios = require("axios");
require("dotenv").config();

const app = express();
app.use(bodyParser.json());

const PORT = process.env.PORT || 5000;

// OpenAI API Call
app.post("/chatbot", async (req, res) => {
    const userMessage = req.body.message;

    try {
        const response = await
axios.post("https://api.openai.com/v1/completions", {
            model: "gpt-4",
```

```
        prompt: userMessage,

        max_tokens: 100

    }, {

        headers: { "Authorization": `Bearer
${process.env.OPENAI_API_KEY}` }

    });


        res.json({ reply: response.data.choices[0].text.trim()
});

    } catch (error) {

        res.status(500).json({ error: "Error processing
chatbot request" });

    }

});


app.listen(PORT, () => console.log(`Chatbot running on port
${PORT}`));
```

Step 3: Connect the Chatbot to the Front-End

Use JavaScript to send messages to the chatbot and display responses.

html

CopyEdit

```
<!DOCTYPE html>

<html lang="en">
```

64

```html
<head>
    <title>AI Chatbot</title>
    <script>
        async function sendMessage() {
            const userInput =
document.getElementById("userInput").value;
            const response = await fetch("/chatbot", {
                method: "POST",
                headers: { "Content-Type": "application/json"
},
                body: JSON.stringify({ message: userInput })
            });
            const data = await response.json();
            document.getElementById("chat").innerHTML +=
`<p>User: ${userInput}</p><p>Bot: ${data.reply}</p>`;
        }
    </script>
</head>
<body>
    <h1>AI Chatbot</h1>
    <div id="chat"></div>
    <input type="text" id="userInput" placeholder="Type a
message">
    <button onclick="sendMessage()">Send</button>
```

```
</body>

</html>
```

Building an AI Chatbot in Python

Python is widely used for **AI development**, offering powerful NLP and ML frameworks such as **NLTK, TensorFlow, and OpenAI API**.

1. Setting Up a Python Chatbot with Flask and OpenAI GPT-4

Step 1: Install Required Libraries

bash

CopyEdit

```
pip install flask openai requests
```

Step 2: Create a Flask API for Chatbot Responses

python

CopyEdit

```python
from flask import Flask, request, jsonify

import openai

import os


app = Flask(__name__)


openai.api_key = os.getenv("OPENAI_API_KEY")
```

```python
@app.route("/chatbot", methods=["POST"])

def chatbot():

    user_message = request.json["message"]


    response = openai.ChatCompletion.create(

        model="gpt-4",

        messages=[{"role": "user", "content": user_message}]

    )


    return jsonify({"reply": response["choices"][0]["message"]["content"]})


if __name__ == "__main__":

    app.run(port=5000, debug=True)
```

Step 3: Create a Simple Web UI for the Python Chatbot

Use Flask with a simple HTML front-end to interact with the chatbot.

html

CopyEdit

```html
<!DOCTYPE html>

<html lang="en">

<head>
```

```html
<title>Python AI Chatbot</title>

<script>

    async function sendMessage() {

        const userInput =
document.getElementById("userInput").value;

        const response = await fetch("/chatbot", {

            method: "POST",

            headers: { "Content-Type": "application/json" },

            body: JSON.stringify({ message: userInput })

        });

        const data = await response.json();

        document.getElementById("chat").innerHTML +=
`<p>User: ${userInput}</p><p>Bot: ${data.reply}</p>`;

    }

</script>

</head>

<body>

    <h1>AI Chatbot</h1>

    <div id="chat"></div>

    <input type="text" id="userInput" placeholder="Type a
message">

    <button onclick="sendMessage()">Send</button>

</body>
```

```
</html>
```

This Python chatbot integrates **OpenAI's GPT-4 API**, enabling dynamic and **context-aware** responses.

Improving Customer Experience with AI-Powered Support Systems

How AI Enhances Customer Support

AI-powered support systems **increase efficiency, reduce response times, and improve customer satisfaction** by automating interactions, providing personalized responses, and learning from past interactions.

1. AI-Powered Automated Ticketing Systems

AI chatbots integrate with **customer support ticketing systems** to:

- Classify and prioritize **customer issues automatically**.
- Assign tickets to **relevant support agents** based on urgency.
- Offer **instant resolutions** to common problems, reducing workload.

Example:

- **Zendesk AI Chatbots** analyze **support tickets and auto-resolve common inquiries**.

2. AI-Driven Sentiment Analysis for Customer Queries

AI-powered **sentiment analysis tools** detect customer emotions and classify messages into **positive, neutral, or negative** sentiments.

How it Works:

1. AI analyzes **tone, word choice, and sentence structure**.
2. Positive sentiments trigger **reward-based interactions** (e.g., discounts, thank-you messages).
3. Negative sentiments **escalate to human agents** for quick intervention.

69

- **IBM Watson AI Support** identifies **frustrated users** and routes them to priority support.

---

3. AI-Powered Live Chat Support with Human-AI Handoff

AI chatbots handle **basic queries**, while **complex issues are forwarded to human agents** for resolution.

Benefits:

- Reduces human workload by **filtering common questions**.
- Improves **response times and efficiency**.
- Ensures **seamless transition** between AI and human support.

Example:

- **Intercom AI Chatbot** provides **automated responses**, but escalates **technical issues to live agents**.

---

4. AI-Driven Voice Assistants for Customer Support

AI-powered voice assistants enhance **call centers and voice-based customer interactions**.

Features:

- Supports **multilingual conversations**.
- Handles **complex queries using NLP**.
- Provides **real-time speech-to-text transcription** for analysis.

Example:

- **Google's Contact Center AI** assists **call center agents by suggesting responses based on real-time analysis**.

AI chatbots and virtual assistants **redefine customer experience** by providing **instant, intelligent, and personalized support**. Implementing AI-powered support systems in **JavaScript and Python** enables businesses to **automate interactions, improve response times, and enhance user engagement**.

By integrating AI-driven customer service tools like **Dialogflow, OpenAI GPT-4, and IBM Watson**, companies can **enhance user satisfaction, streamline operations, and scale their support capabilities** effortlessly.

Chapter 6

AI-Based Content Generation and SEO Optimization

How AI Enhances Content Creation and Blogging

Introduction to AI in Content Creation

Content creation has evolved from **manual writing** to **AI-assisted automation**, where artificial intelligence generates, enhances, and optimizes content **faster, more accurately, and with better audience targeting**. AI-powered tools **assist bloggers, marketers, and businesses** in crafting high-quality content by using **natural language processing (NLP), deep learning, and machine learning algorithms**.

AI-driven content creation improves efficiency by **automating research, topic suggestions, content structuring, and even writing**. With platforms like **OpenAI's GPT-4, Jasper AI, and Copy.ai**, writers can produce engaging articles, blogs, and marketing copy with **minimal effort** while maintaining a **human-like tone and readability**.

---

1. AI's Role in Content Creation for Blogs and Websites

AI enhances blogging by:

- **Generating high-quality articles** in seconds.
- **Optimizing headlines, keywords, and readability**.
- **Automating topic research** based on trends.
- **Improving grammar, tone, and coherence**.
- **Personalizing content** for different audiences.

How AI Generates Content

AI-based content creation involves a series of automated steps to **write well-structured, engaging, and SEO-friendly articles**:

1. **Topic Research & Ideation**

   - AI analyzes **search trends, competitor blogs, and industry news** to suggest topics.
   - Tools like **BuzzSumo and Google Trends** track trending topics for content planning.

2. **AI-Powered Content Outlining**

   - AI suggests **headings, subheadings, and paragraph structures** to improve organization.
   - Platforms like **Frase and Clearscope** help optimize outlines based on SEO strategies.

3. **AI-Generated Drafts**

   - AI writing assistants **produce article drafts** with coherent introductions, body content, and conclusions.
   - OpenAI's **GPT-4** and **Jasper AI** generate blog posts with minimal input.

4. **Grammar & Readability Enhancement**

   - AI refines **grammar, spelling, tone, and clarity**.
   - Tools like **Grammarly and Hemingway Editor** enhance sentence structure for better readability.

5. **SEO Optimization**

   - AI suggests **relevant keywords, meta descriptions, and backlinks**.
   - AI-powered tools like **Surfer SEO and Clearscope** analyze **SEO score and readability**.

6. **Personalization & Audience Targeting**

   - AI personalizes blog content based on user **preferences, location, and engagement history**.
   - AI-powered CMS systems **adapt blog content dynamically for different audiences**.

---

2. AI-Based Content Generation Tools

AI Tool	Function	Use Case
Jasper AI	AI-driven long-form blog writing	Automated article generation
Copy.ai	AI-powered copywriting for marketing	Social media posts, ad copy
Frase	AI-driven SEO content research	Topic & keyword optimization
Rytr AI	AI-based writing assistant	Blog writing & product descriptions
Gramm arly	AI grammar & readability check	Proofreading & tone improvement

3. AI's Impact on Blogging Efficiency

AI reduces **time spent on writing, editing, and optimizing content**, allowing bloggers and businesses to focus on **engagement and monetization strategies**.

Benefits of AI for Blogging

Benefit	Description
Faster Content Production	AI writes **blogs in minutes**, saving time.
Higher SEO Rankings	AI optimizes **keywords, meta tags, and readability**.

74

Personalized User Experience	AI generates **customized content** based on user behavior.
Better Engagement	AI-driven content **keeps readers engaged with optimized structures**.

With AI's assistance, businesses and bloggers **create engaging, high-quality, and SEO-optimized content** that attracts traffic and improves conversions.

AI-Powered SEO Tools: Google BERT, Surfer SEO, and Clearscope

Search Engine Optimization (SEO) is **critical for driving organic traffic** to websites. AI has revolutionized SEO by **enhancing keyword research, optimizing content, and improving user search intent understanding**.

1. Google BERT: AI for Search Understanding

Google BERT (**Bidirectional Encoder Representations from Transformers**) is an **AI-powered search algorithm** that helps Google understand:

- **Context and intent** behind search queries.
- **User behavior and engagement patterns**.
- **Natural language nuances in web content**.

How Google BERT Enhances SEO

1. **Improves Search Query Understanding**

   - BERT enables Google to **interpret long-tail keywords** more accurately.
   - Focuses on **meaning over exact keyword matching**.
2. **Ranks High-Quality Content**

   - Google prioritizes **well-written, context-rich articles**.

○ Poorly structured, keyword-stuffed content is **penalized**.
3. **Better Voice Search Results**

   ○ AI-powered **voice search** queries require **conversational content**.
   ○ BERT improves **understanding of natural spoken queries**.

Example:

A traditional keyword search might rank "Best smartphones 2025," while BERT understands **longer, more natural queries** like:
"What are the best budget smartphones under $500 in 2025?"

---

2. Surfer SEO: AI-Powered On-Page Optimization

Surfer SEO is an **AI-driven tool** that helps businesses optimize web content based on **real-time SEO analysis**.

Key Features of Surfer SEO

Feature	Function
Content Score	Grades content based on **SEO-friendly writing**.
Keyword Analysis	Identifies **optimal keywords & LSI terms**.
Competitor Analysis	Compares **top-ranking websites for keyword insights**.
SEO-Driven Outlines	Provides **structured blog templates** for SEO ranking.

How Surfer SEO Improves Search Rankings

1. **Analyzes competitor content** to identify **gaps and ranking opportunities**.

2. **Suggests real-time keyword usage** to improve visibility.
3. **Optimizes structure, word count, and readability** for Google ranking.

Example:

A website using Surfer SEO **adjusts blog content dynamically** to match top-ranking articles, improving its chances of ranking on **Google's first page**.

3. Clearscope: AI-Driven Content Optimization

Clearscope is an **AI-powered SEO tool** that enhances content relevance by providing:

- **Keyword recommendations based on search intent.**
- **Content grading system to evaluate SEO effectiveness.**
- **Topic suggestions to improve depth and coverage.**

How Clearscope Works

1. **Scans high-ranking pages** for a keyword.
2. **Suggests related terms** that improve ranking potential.
3. **Assigns content scores** based on how well articles match **Google's top results**.

Example:

A blog post optimized with Clearscope **outperforms generic content** by aligning with **Google's search intent**, leading to **higher traffic and engagement**.

Comparing AI-Powered SEO Tools

Feature	Google BERT	Surfer SEO	Clearscope
Function	AI search algorithm	AI-based on-page SEO optimization	AI-powered content scoring

Focus	Search intent understanding	Real-time keyword & structure suggestions	Keyword & content relevance analysis
Ideal for	Bloggers, websites with long-form content	Content marketers, SEO agencies	Enterprise businesses, high-ranking content strategies

AI-powered SEO tools like **Google BERT, Surfer SEO, and Clearscope** help **automate and optimize** search ranking strategies, making it easier for websites to **attract organic traffic and stay competitive**.

AI is transforming **content creation and SEO optimization**, enabling websites and businesses to **automate blog writing, enhance search rankings, and drive user engagement**. AI-powered tools like **Google BERT, Surfer SEO, and Clearscope** ensure that content remains **high-quality, search-friendly, and tailored to user intent**.

By integrating AI into blogging and SEO, businesses can **increase visibility, improve content strategy, and maintain a competitive edge in digital marketing**.

AI-Driven Keyword Research and SEO Audits

Introduction to AI in Keyword Research and SEO Audits

Search Engine Optimization (SEO) is critical for any website that aims to **attract organic traffic** and improve its search ranking. Traditional keyword research and SEO audits required **manual effort, spreadsheets, and trial-and-error approaches**, but AI has completely transformed these processes.

AI-driven keyword research and SEO audits leverage **machine learning, predictive analytics, and natural language processing (NLP)** to identify **high-ranking keywords, optimize website content, and detect SEO issues** faster and more accurately than ever before.

1. AI in Keyword Research

How AI Enhances Keyword Research

AI-powered keyword research tools analyze **search intent, user behavior, and competitor strategies** to suggest **the most effective keywords** for content ranking.

Key AI functionalities for keyword research include:

- **Understanding Search Intent** – AI categorizes keywords based on **informational, transactional, and navigational intent**.
- **Predicting Keyword Trends** – AI models forecast **rising search trends** before they peak.
- **Competitor Analysis** – AI scans **top-ranking websites** to identify **high-performing keywords**.
- **Long-Tail Keyword Discovery** – AI recommends **long-tail, low-competition keywords** that drive targeted traffic.

AI-Powered Keyword Research Tools

Tool	Function	Example Use Case
Google Keyword Planner AI	Suggests **high-ranking keywords** based on search trends.	Optimizing Google Ads & SEO campaigns.
SEMrush AI	Provides **keyword difficulty analysis & competitor research**.	Finding long-tail keywords to outrank competitors.
Ahrefs AI	Tracks **keyword ranking potential & backlink analysis**.	Building SEO strategies for authority sites.
Surfer SEO	AI-powered keyword clustering and content strategy.	Creating keyword-optimized blog outlines.

2. AI in SEO Audits

AI-powered SEO audits **automate website analysis** by identifying **technical issues, content gaps, and optimization opportunities**. AI-driven audits provide:

1. **On-Page SEO Analysis**

   o Detects **broken links, missing meta descriptions, duplicate content, and poor site structure**.
   o AI suggests **content improvements for better readability and keyword density**.

2. **Technical SEO Checks**

   o Identifies **crawl errors, indexing problems, and page speed issues**.
   o AI-enhanced tools like **Google Lighthouse** analyze **Core Web Vitals** for UX improvement.

3. **AI-Powered Backlink Analysis**

   o AI tools **monitor backlink quality**, detecting **toxic links that harm rankings**.
   o Helps websites **build high-authority links** using predictive recommendations.

4. **Competitor SEO Benchmarking**

   o AI scans **top-ranking competitors** and highlights **SEO strategies to outrank them**.
   o Compares **keyword usage, content length, and backlink profiles**.

AI-Powered SEO Audit Tools

Tool	Function	Example Use Case
Google Search Console AI	Identifies **indexing issues and performance metrics**.	Resolving broken links and sitemap errors.

80

Screaming Frog AI SEO Spider	Crawls websites for **SEO errors & optimization tips**.	Improving technical SEO & fixing on-page issues.
Moz Pro AI	Conducts **site audits, domain authority tracking, and link analysis**.	Enhancing overall SEO health.
SEMrush Site Audit AI	Provides **AI-powered SEO error detection and fixes**.	Optimizing web pages for higher rankings.

Automating Content Optimization for Search Engines

Introduction to AI-Driven Content Optimization

Creating SEO-friendly content involves **more than just keyword stuffing**. AI automates content optimization by:

- **Analyzing search engine algorithms** to improve content structure.
- **Ensuring proper keyword density** without overuse.
- **Suggesting readability improvements** to enhance user engagement.
- **Generating meta tags, alt text, and schema markup** automatically.

1. AI in Content Optimization for SEO

AI-powered content optimization involves several key techniques:

1. **Keyword Integration & Natural Language Flow**

   o AI ensures **keywords are naturally embedded** in the text without disrupting readability.
   o NLP-based tools like **Google's RankBrain** prioritize **context over keyword frequency**.

2. **AI-Powered Readability Enhancements**

   o AI tools assess **Flesch-Kincaid readability scores** and suggest simpler phrasing.
   o AI-based platforms like **Hemingway Editor** refine sentence structures.

3. **Automated Meta Description & Schema Markup**

   o AI generates **SEO-friendly meta descriptions** tailored to Google's snippet guidelines.
   o AI tools like **Merkle Schema Generator** add **structured data for better visibility**.

4. **Real-Time SEO Suggestions**

   o AI-driven platforms like **Surfer SEO and Clearscope** provide **live content feedback** while writing.
   o AI highlights **missing keywords, readability issues, and competitor comparisons**.

---

2. AI Tools for Automated Content Optimization

Tool	Function	Example Use Case
Frase AI	Optimizes content with **real-time topic analysis**.	Improving blog post SEO structure.
MarketM use AI	AI-driven **content gap analysis & strategy**.	Identifying missing subtopics for better rankings.
Surfer SEO	AI-based **on-page optimization & ranking predictions**.	Real-time content grading & improvement.

Clearsco pe AI	NLP-powered **content relevance analysis**.	Optimizing articles to match Google's top-ranking content.

3. AI-Powered Content Refresh Strategies

AI also helps **revive old content** to improve search rankings:

1. **AI Detects Outdated Content**

   - AI tracks **declining traffic and search performance** of old articles.
   - Tools like **Google Search Console AI** suggest content updates.

2. **AI Rewrites & Enhances Existing Blogs**

   - AI rephrases content **to align with current SEO trends**.
   - Tools like **Jasper AI and Rytr** generate **new sections based on updated search intent**.

3. **AI-Powered Image & Video Optimization**

   - AI compresses images and **suggests alt-text for better indexing**.
   - AI platforms like **Cloudinary** optimize visual assets **without quality loss**.

The Future of AI-Driven Content and SEO

With AI continually evolving, the future of **AI-powered SEO and content optimization** will include:

- **Voice Search Optimization** → AI will prioritize **natural speech patterns** for voice search rankings.
- **AI-Powered Video SEO** → AI will **transcribe, tag, and analyze** video content for better search visibility.
- **Predictive SEO Analytics** → AI will anticipate **ranking fluctuations and content trends** before they happen.

AI has **revolutionized keyword research, SEO audits, and content optimization**, making SEO processes **more accurate, efficient, and scalable**. By leveraging AI-powered tools like **Surfer SEO, Clearscope, Google BERT, and SEMrush**, businesses and bloggers can **automate SEO strategies, improve search rankings, and drive higher organic traffic**.

AI-driven automation ensures that content remains **highly relevant, search-friendly, and continuously optimized for search engines**, helping websites **stay competitive in an evolving digital landscape**.

Chapter 7

Automating Backend Processes with AI

AI for Data Processing and Form Validation

Introduction to AI in Backend Automation

Backend systems form the **foundation of web applications**, handling **data processing, validation, storage, and workflow automation**. Traditionally, backend processes required **manual coding, database queries, and rule-based validation**. However, AI-driven automation is transforming backend development by **enhancing efficiency, reducing human error, and optimizing performance**.

AI-powered backend systems automate **data processing, form validation, CRUD operations, and database management**, allowing developers to build **scalable, intelligent, and self-learning applications**.

---

1. AI for Data Processing in Backend Systems

AI is revolutionizing **data processing** by automating **data cleaning, transformation, and analysis**. AI-based backend systems process **large-scale data with minimal human intervention**, ensuring **higher accuracy and faster execution**.

How AI Enhances Data Processing in Backend Workflows

AI Feature	Function	Example Use Case
AI-Powered Data Cleansing	Detects and removes duplicates, incorrect	AI auto-correcting incorrect customer

	formatting, and missing values.	details in CRM systems.
AI-Based Data Classification	Categorizes and labels incoming data using ML models.	AI sorting incoming email messages into "spam," "urgent," and "normal."
Predictive Data Analytics	AI identifies patterns and trends for business insights.	AI predicting **customer churn rates** based on behavior.
Automated Data Transformatio n	Converts raw data into structured formats for database storage.	AI converting **raw JSON logs into a structured SQL format**.

2. AI for Form Validation and User Input Processing

Form validation ensures that user inputs are **correct, complete, and secure** before submission to the backend. AI-based form validation replaces **traditional rule-based validation** by learning from **user behavior, past errors, and security threats** to **intelligently correct and validate form submissions**.

AI-Driven Form Validation Techniques

1. **AI-Powered Data Validation**

   - Detects typos, incorrect formats, and missing fields.
   - Uses machine learning to **predict and auto-correct form inputs**.
2. **AI-Based Fraud Detection in Forms**

   - Identifies fraudulent patterns and blocks suspicious submissions.
   - Uses **CAPTCHA-less validation** to differentiate humans from bots.

3. **AI for Real-Time Auto-Suggestions**

    ○ Suggests valid inputs based on **past user behavior**.
    ○ Provides **real-time address correction and autocomplete suggestions**.

Examples of AI in Form Validation

Feature	AI Function	Example
Auto-Correct	AI fixes incorrect entries automatically.	Fixing misspelled email addresses in registration forms.
Intelligent Auto-Fill	Suggests relevant data based on history.	AI predicting **city and ZIP code** based on street address.
Behavior-Based Validation	Detects bot-like behavior to prevent spam.	AI blocking fraudulent sign-ups on financial apps.
ML-Based Input Detection	Learns user preferences to validate fields.	AI identifying **invalid phone numbers** before submission.

By integrating **AI-powered form validation**, backend systems reduce **human errors, improve security, and enhance user experience**.

AI-Driven CRUD Operations and Database Management

Introduction to AI-Powered Database Management

CRUD (Create, Read, Update, Delete) operations are the **foundation of database management**. AI-driven automation enhances CRUD operations by:

- Reducing manual SQL queries with intelligent data retrieval systems.
- Optimizing database performance through AI-driven indexing and query optimization.
- Automating anomaly detection and security measures in data transactions.

---

1. AI-Powered CRUD Operations

AI enhances CRUD operations in the backend by **optimizing database interactions, improving query efficiency, and ensuring data integrity**.

How AI Optimizes CRUD Operations

AI Feature	Function	Example
AI-Based Query Optimization	Enhances SQL query efficiency using ML models.	AI improving query execution time in e-commerce databases.
Automated Data Pre-Fetching	Predicts and loads frequently accessed data.	AI preloading user profile details for faster access.
AI-Powered Auto-Scaling	Adjusts database capacity dynamically.	AI optimizing database load during high-traffic events.

| AI-Driven Data Replication | Automates data backups and replication. | AI managing **cloud-based database backups** in real-time. |

---

2. AI for Intelligent Database Management

AI automates **database maintenance, indexing, and security monitoring**, making backend processes **more efficient and self-optimizing**.

AI-Powered Database Management Techniques

1. **AI-Based Indexing and Query Optimization**

   o AI **automatically adjusts indexing strategies** based on usage patterns.
   o Predictive AI **suggests optimal indexing methods** to reduce latency.
2. **Automated Data Consistency and Anomaly Detection**

   o AI detects and resolves **data inconsistencies across multiple tables**.
   o AI-driven anomaly detection prevents **unauthorized data modifications**.
3. **Self-Healing Databases with AI**

   o AI monitors database **health, identifies failures, and triggers automatic repairs**.
   o **Google's Cloud Spanner** uses AI for **real-time database optimization**.

Examples of AI in Database Management

Feature	AI Function	Example
Intelligent Query Execution	AI predicts and optimizes queries dynamically.	AI-enhanced MySQL query execution for faster processing.

Database Auto-Tuning	AI adjusts memory allocation and indexing strategies.	AI optimizing **PostgreSQL performance based on usage trends**.
Self-Healing Databases	AI automatically fixes corruption or failures.	AI-driven **Amazon Aurora database recovery**.

By leveraging AI, **backend database operations become faster, more secure, and self-optimizing**, reducing **manual effort and operational costs**.

How AI Helps in Automating Backend Workflows

1. AI-Powered Task Automation in Backend Systems

AI streamlines backend workflows by automating **repetitive tasks, monitoring system performance, and making real-time adjustments**.

AI-Powered Automation	Function	Example
Automated API Management	AI handles API request routing and caching.	AI optimizing **GraphQL query responses**.
AI-Based Load Balancing	AI distributes traffic intelligently across servers.	AI-powered **AWS Auto Scaling**.
Automated System Monitoring	AI detects anomalies and sends alerts.	AI-powered **real-time error reporting in DevOps**.

| Predictive Maintenance | AI forecasts system failures before they happen. | AI-driven **cloud infrastructure monitoring**. |

2. AI in Task Scheduling and Job Execution

AI enhances backend job execution by **predicting optimal execution times and prioritizing tasks dynamically**.

AI Function	Description	Example
Smart Task Scheduling	AI predicts when tasks should run based on server load.	AI adjusting **database backups to low-traffic hours**.
Event-Driven Automation	AI triggers actions based on system events.	AI-driven **automated report generation** when new data arrives.
Real-Time API Optimization	AI auto-adjusts API response time based on request patterns.	AI enhancing **RESTful API efficiency for SaaS platforms**.

The Future of AI-Driven Backend Automation

AI will continue to **redefine backend automation**, integrating with **cloud computing, DevOps, and security** to create **self-learning, fully automated infrastructures**.

Upcoming AI Trends in Backend Automation

- **AI-Powered DevOps Pipelines** → AI-driven **continuous integration & deployment (CI/CD)**.

91

- **Serverless AI Architectures** → AI will **optimize cloud computing resources dynamically**.
- **AI-Enhanced Cybersecurity** → AI will detect and prevent **backend security threats in real-time**.

AI-powered backend automation **transforms web development by automating data processing, database management, form validation, and workflow execution**. By leveraging AI-driven tools, developers can build **self-sustaining, intelligent, and highly efficient backend systems** that **enhance performance, scalability, and security**.

Chapter 8

AI for Web Security and Threat Detection

AI in Cybersecurity for Web Applications

Introduction to AI in Cybersecurity

As web applications become more sophisticated, they also become **prime targets for cyber threats, data breaches, and malicious attacks**. Traditional security measures like **rule-based firewalls and manual threat detection** are no longer sufficient to combat advanced cyber threats. This is where **Artificial Intelligence (AI) and Machine Learning (ML)** play a crucial role in **automating security, detecting anomalies, and mitigating risks in real-time**.

AI-driven cybersecurity enhances **threat detection, data encryption, user authentication, fraud prevention, and malware identification**, making web applications **more resilient against cyberattacks**.

---

1. AI's Role in Web Application Security

AI-powered security solutions leverage **machine learning, deep learning, and behavior analytics** to enhance web security in the following ways:

AI Security Function	How It Works	Example
AI-Based Intrusion Detection	AI monitors web traffic and detects **suspicious behavior in real time**.	AI detects **SQL injection attacks on login pages**.

Behavioral Threat Analysis	AI learns user behavior patterns and **flags unusual activities**.	AI detects **unauthorized admin login attempts**.
Automated Malware Detection	AI scans web applications for **malicious scripts and vulnerabilities**.	AI detects **JavaScript malware embedded in website code**.
AI-Powered Encryption & Authentication	AI enhances **password security, two-factor authentication (2FA), and biometrics**.	AI-powered **facial recognition login for e-commerce sites**.
Cloud Security with AI	AI protects **cloud-hosted applications** by monitoring network traffic and APIs.	AI detects **unauthorized API access in cloud environments**.

AI-driven security ensures **faster threat response, improved accuracy, and reduced reliance on manual monitoring**.

---

2. AI-Powered Cyber Threat Intelligence

How AI Helps in Threat Intelligence and Response

Cyber Threat Intelligence (CTI) uses AI to **gather, analyze, and respond** to security threats proactively. AI-driven CTI systems:

- **Collect data** from multiple threat intelligence sources.
- **Analyze attack patterns** to predict **potential security breaches**.
- **Automate security responses** to mitigate risks before they escalate.

Examples of AI in Cyber Threat Intelligence

AI-Powered Threat Intelligence	Function	Example
AI-Driven Honeypots	AI detects hackers by setting up fake networks.	AI baiting **attackers with decoy credentials**.
Automated Phishing Detection	AI scans emails and websites for phishing indicators.	AI blocking **malicious email attachments and fake login pages**.
AI-Powered Ransomware Protection	AI detects ransomware behavior **before encryption occurs**.	AI stopping **malicious file execution in real time**.
AI for DNS Security	AI identifies and blocks **malicious domains and IP addresses**.	AI preventing **access to phishing websites**.

By leveraging AI for cyber threat intelligence, businesses can **prevent security breaches before they occur, ensuring a proactive security approach**.

Machine Learning Models for Detecting Threats

1. How Machine Learning Enhances Threat Detection

Machine Learning (ML) models improve cybersecurity by **identifying patterns in vast amounts of data, detecting anomalies, and adapting to new threats**. Unlike traditional security systems that rely on **static rule sets**, ML models **learn from past attacks and continuously refine their detection capabilities**.

Types of Machine Learning Models Used in Web Security

ML Model	Function	Example Use Case
Supervised Learning	Trains on labeled threat data to detect known attacks.	AI flagging **previously identified malware signatures**.
Unsupervised Learning	Identifies new threats based on anomalous patterns.	AI detecting **new zero-day attacks**.
Reinforcement Learning	Learns from real-time security feedback to improve detection.	AI improving **firewall accuracy over time**.
Deep Learning (Neural Networks)	Identifies complex attack patterns with high accuracy.	AI recognizing **hidden malware behaviors**.

---

2. AI-Powered Anomaly Detection in Web Security

AI-driven anomaly detection identifies **unusual activities that indicate security threats**.

How AI Detects Anomalies in Web Applications

- **AI monitors user behavior** (e.g., login times, IP addresses, browser types).
- **Detects unusual patterns**, such as a **user logging in from multiple locations in a short time**.
- **Flags suspicious API requests** that deviate from normal traffic patterns.

96

Real-World Applications of AI in Anomaly Detection

AI Security Feature	How It Works	Example
AI-Based User Behavior Analysis	Detects unauthorized access attempts.	AI blocking **fraudulent logins from new devices**.
AI for Bot Detection	Identifies **malicious bot traffic** on websites.	AI blocking **DDoS attacks on e-commerce sites**.
AI-Powered API Security	Prevents API misuse and attacks.	AI detecting **API scraping attempts on a SaaS platform**.

AI-powered threat detection ensures **faster incident response, reduced false positives, and enhanced security accuracy**.

AI-Based Fraud Prevention and Spam Detection

1. AI in Online Fraud Prevention

Fraud detection in web applications is essential for **preventing financial losses, identity theft, and unauthorized transactions**. AI uses **machine learning and behavioral analytics** to identify and block fraudulent activities in real time.

How AI Prevents Fraud in Web Applications

AI Function	How It Works	Example

AI-Powered Transaction Monitoring	Analyzes **payment behavior** for fraud indicators.	AI detecting **credit card fraud in online stores**.
Device & IP Fingerprinting	Identifies unusual device activity.	AI blocking **multiple transactions from different locations within minutes**.
Behavioral Biometrics	Uses AI to **analyze user behavior patterns**.	AI detecting **fake account registrations**.
Automated Chargeback Prevention	AI predicts **fraudulent refund requests**.	AI blocking **abuse of return policies in e-commerce**.

By integrating AI into fraud prevention, businesses **protect users, reduce losses, and improve transaction security**.

---

2. AI for Spam and Phishing Detection

AI plays a crucial role in **identifying spam messages, fraudulent emails, and phishing attempts**.

How AI Detects Spam and Phishing Attacks

1. **AI scans email headers, content, and sender reputation**.
2. **Identifies spam patterns and malicious links**.
3. **Uses NLP to analyze email intent**.
4. **Prevents users from clicking on phishing links**.

AI-Powered Spam Detection Tools

Tool	Function	Example
Google Spam AI	Blocks spam emails automatically.	Gmail AI filtering **fraudulent emails**.
Akismet AI	AI-based spam detection for websites.	Blocking **spam comments on blogs**.
Microsoft Defender AI	Identifies phishing websites.	AI blocking **fake login pages**.

AI-driven spam detection ensures **higher security, better email filtering, and reduced phishing risks**.

AI-powered cybersecurity is essential for **detecting and preventing threats in web applications**. By leveraging **machine learning models, anomaly detection, fraud prevention, and automated security responses**, businesses can **stay ahead of cybercriminals and ensure a secure digital environment**.

With AI continuously evolving, the future of **web security will rely on self-learning AI systems that predict and neutralize threats before they cause harm**.

Chapter 9

AI-Powered Search and Recommendation Systems

AI-Driven Search Algorithms for Web Applications

Introduction to AI-Powered Search

Search functionality is a crucial component of modern web applications, enabling users to **retrieve relevant information efficiently**. Traditional search algorithms rely on **keyword matching and indexing techniques**, but they often fail to understand **user intent, context, and personalized preferences**.

AI-powered search engines **enhance accuracy, relevance, and speed** by incorporating **Natural Language Processing (NLP), Machine Learning (ML), and Deep Learning**. These AI-driven approaches enable:

- **Semantic search** that understands user intent rather than relying on exact keyword matches.
- **Personalized search recommendations** based on user behavior.
- **Voice and image-based search functionalities**.
- **Real-time indexing and predictive search suggestions**.

---

1. AI Techniques Used in Search Algorithms

AI Search Technique	Function	Example Use Case
Semantic Search with NLP	Understands query context rather than just keywords.	AI detecting synonyms and meaning variations in search queries.

Machine Learning-Bas ed Ranking	Adjusts search rankings based on user interaction history.	AI optimizing product search results in e-commerce.
AI-Powered Query Expansion	Suggests related terms and expands search queries.	Google Suggest refining search terms dynamically.
Voice Search Recognition	Uses AI to process spoken queries.	AI-powered voice search in smart assistants (Alexa, Google Assistant).
Image-Based Search	AI recognizes and searches for visual elements.	Google Lens identifying objects from images.

2. Semantic Search and AI-Driven Ranking

AI-driven search systems improve **search result accuracy** by incorporating:

1. **Natural Language Understanding (NLU)**

   - Detects **intent and meaning** behind queries.
   - Helps differentiate between ambiguous words (e.g., "apple" as a fruit vs. the company Apple).

2. **AI-Based Query Processing**

   - Uses **Named Entity Recognition (NER)** to extract specific entities like **dates, locations, or product names**.
   - Handles **spelling errors, typos, and slang** effectively.

3. **Machine Learning for Personalized Ranking**

   - AI adjusts search rankings based on **user behavior and preferences**.

- Amazon's AI search algorithm ranks products higher based on purchase history.

---

3. AI-Powered Search Applications

Industry	AI Search Use Case	Example
E-Commerce	Personalized product search and filtering.	AI-driven search on Amazon and eBay.
Healthcare	AI-powered medical research and drug discovery.	AI search in IBM Watson for health research.
Education	AI-driven knowledge search in learning platforms.	Google AI-enhanced search for research papers.
Entertainment	Smart search and content recommendations.	Netflix AI-based movie search suggestions.

By integrating **AI-driven search algorithms**, web applications improve **user experience, engagement, and information retrieval efficiency**.

Implementing Elasticsearch with AI Enhancements

1. What is Elasticsearch?

Elasticsearch is a **distributed search and analytics engine** designed for **full-text search, log analytics, and real-time data retrieval**. It is widely used in **enterprise search, e-commerce, and large-scale web applications**.

Elasticsearch supports **AI-driven enhancements** to optimize:

102

- Query relevance ranking using ML models.
- Context-aware search and auto-suggestions.
- Personalized search recommendations.

2. Integrating AI with Elasticsearch

AI enhances Elasticsearch by **analyzing user behavior, predicting intent, and refining search results dynamically**.

How AI Enhances Elasticsearch

AI Feature	Function	Example Use Case
Machine Learning-Base d Ranking	Adjusts search rankings dynamically based on user interaction.	AI ranking frequently searched items higher.
Natural Language Query Processing	Converts unstructured queries into structured search commands.	AI-powered voice-to-text search queries.
Query Expansion & Auto-Suggesti ons	Predicts and recommends search phrases dynamically.	AI-powered Google Autocomplete.
Real-Time Search Optimization	AI-driven adjustments for trending search terms.	E-commerce sites promoting seasonal products dynamically.

3. Example: Implementing AI-Powered Elasticsearch

Step 1: Setting Up Elasticsearch

bash

CopyEdit

```
docker run -d -p 9200:9200 -e "discovery.type=single-node"
elasticsearch:7.10.0
```

Step 2: Indexing Data with AI-Based Ranking

json

CopyEdit

```
PUT /products/_doc/1

{

  "name": "Wireless Headphones",

  "description": "Noise-canceling over-ear headphones with AI
assistant",

  "category": "Electronics",

  "search_rank": 9.8

}
```

Step 3: Implementing AI-Based Query Suggestions

json

CopyEdit

```
GET /products/_search

{

  "query": {
```

```
    "match": {

      "name": "headphones"

    }

  },

  "suggest": {

    "text": "wirless hedphones",

    "term": {

      "field": "name"

    }

  }

}
```

This implementation uses **AI-driven auto-correction and relevance ranking** to **optimize search results dynamically.**

Building AI-Powered Recommendation Systems for E-Commerce

1. The Role of AI in Recommendation Engines

AI-driven recommendation systems analyze **user behavior, preferences, and purchasing history** to **suggest relevant products, movies, or content.** These systems increase **engagement, conversions, and user satisfaction.**

2. Types of AI-Based Recommendation Systems

AI Model	Function	Example Use Case
Content-Based Filtering	Suggests similar items based on past user behavior.	Amazon recommending related books based on purchase history.
Collaborative Filtering	Uses **crowdsourced user preferences** to recommend items.	Netflix suggesting movies based on similar users' watch history.
Hybrid Recommendatio n System	Combines content-based and collaborative filtering.	YouTube's AI recommending videos based on views and watch time.
Deep Learning-Based Personalization	Uses deep learning to predict user preferences dynamically.	AI curating playlists on Spotify.

---

3. Implementing AI-Based Recommendation Systems

Step 1: Data Collection

- Gather **user interaction data** (e.g., clicks, views, purchases).
- Store historical **browsing behavior**.

Step 2: AI Model Training (Collaborative Filtering Example in Python)

python

CopyEdit

106

```
import pandas as pd

from surprise import SVD

from surprise import Dataset

from surprise.model_selection import train_test_split


# Load sample user-product data

data = Dataset.load_builtin('ml-100k')

trainset, testset = train_test_split(data, test_size=0.25)


# Train an AI-powered recommendation model

model = SVD()

model.fit(trainset)


# Generate product recommendations

predictions = model.test(testset)
```

Step 3: Integrating AI Recommendations in Web Applications

- Display **"Recommended for You"** sections based on AI predictions.
- Use **deep learning models** to personalize recommendations in real time.

---

4. AI-Powered Recommendation Systems in Action

Industry	AI Recommendation Use Case	Example

E-Comme rce	AI recommending products based on user history.	Amazon's **"Customers Also Bought" feature.**
Streaming Services	AI suggesting movies, TV shows, and music playlists.	Netflix and Spotify AI-driven recommendations.
News & Media	AI curating personalized articles for readers.	Google News AI-based story suggestions.

AI-powered recommendation systems **increase user engagement, drive sales, and enhance user satisfaction**, making them a crucial feature for e-commerce and content platforms.

AI-driven search and recommendation systems **enhance web application usability, efficiency, and user experience**. By leveraging **Elasticsearch with AI enhancements, machine learning models for ranking, and deep learning-based personalization**, businesses can **deliver smarter search results and tailored recommendations**.

The future of **AI-powered search and recommendations** includes:

- **Voice and AI-driven conversational search**.
- **Hyper-personalized AI recommendations using deep learning**.
- **Real-time adaptive search and ranking optimization**.

By integrating AI, businesses can **increase conversions, improve user engagement, and stay ahead in competitive markets**.

Chapter 10

AI-Powered Performance Optimization

AI for Web Speed and Performance Enhancement

Introduction to AI in Web Performance Optimization

Web performance is a **critical factor** in user experience, search engine ranking, and conversion rates. Slow-loading websites lead to **higher bounce rates, lower engagement, and lost revenue.** Traditionally, optimizing website speed involved **manual performance analysis, code minification, caching, and load balancing.** However, **AI-driven optimization techniques** can now enhance web performance **automatically and dynamically.**

AI improves **web speed and performance** by:

* **Predicting and preventing slowdowns.**
* **Automatically optimizing page load times.**
* **Reducing unnecessary data transfers and script execution.**
* **Balancing server loads and optimizing caching strategies.**

By leveraging **machine learning, predictive analytics, and real-time monitoring,** AI can **boost website performance, ensuring a seamless experience for users.**

---

1. AI Techniques for Web Performance Enhancement

AI Optimization Technique	Function	Example Use Case
AI-Powered Content Delivery	AI caches frequently accessed content and	Cloudflare AI dynamically routing

Networks (CDNs)	optimizes delivery speed.	traffic for faster loading.
Predictive Page Preloading	AI anticipates which pages a user is likely to visit and preloads them.	AI preloading e-commerce product pages based on browsing patterns.
AI-Based Code Minification	AI optimizes JavaScript, CSS, and HTML by removing unnecessary code.	Google AI automatically compressing web scripts for faster execution.
Automated Lazy Loading	AI determines which images and videos should load first.	AI delaying offscreen content loading until needed.
AI-Driven Cache Optimization	AI predicts which data should be stored in cache for optimal speed.	AI-powered edge caching in AWS CloudFront.

These AI-powered optimizations **reduce page load times, improve efficiency, and enhance overall web experience**.

---

2. AI-Powered Content Delivery Networks (CDNs)

A **Content Delivery Network (CDN)** improves website speed by distributing content **across multiple global servers**. AI-driven CDNs optimize:

- **Traffic Routing** → AI determines the **fastest path** to deliver data.
- **Edge Computing** → AI **caches content dynamically** closer to users.
- **Load Balancing** → AI **distributes server load intelligently**.

110

Cloudflare uses AI to:

- **Predict and prevent server congestion.**
- **Reduce latency in content delivery.**
- **Optimize web traffic by identifying the fastest routes.**

By implementing **AI-powered CDNs**, web applications achieve **faster load times, reduced bandwidth usage, and improved reliability**.

AI-Based Image and Video Compression

1. The Role of AI in Media Compression

Images and videos **consume significant bandwidth**, affecting web performance and increasing page load times. Traditional compression techniques often result in **loss of quality**. AI-powered compression **reduces file sizes while maintaining visual clarity**.

AI optimizes image and video compression by:

- **Analyzing and adjusting quality dynamically.**
- **Applying deep learning models to remove unnecessary pixels.**
- **Enhancing compressed images/videos using neural networks.**

2. AI-Powered Image Compression

AI-based image compression tools use **machine learning and neural networks** to optimize image files without **visible quality loss**.

AI Image Optimization Technique	Function	Example Use Case

AI-Based Lossless Compression	Reduces file size without quality degradation.	AI optimizing product images for e-commerce sites.
Neural Network Image Upscaling	Restores compressed images to near-original quality.	AI enhancing thumbnails in streaming platforms.
AI-Driven Format Conversion	Converts images to more efficient formats like WebP.	Google's AI-powered image format conversion.
Adaptive Image Resizing	AI adjusts image resolution dynamically based on device and network speed.	AI scaling images for mobile-first websites.

Example: AI-Optimized Image Compression with TensorFlow

python

CopyEdit

```
import tensorflow as tf

import tensorflow_hub as hub

import cv2


# Load AI-based image compression model
model =
hub.load("https://tfhub.dev/google/imagenet/mobilenet_v2_100_2
24/classification/5")
```

```
# Load and compress image

image = cv2.imread("image.jpg")

compressed_image = cv2.resize(image, (224, 224),
interpolation=cv2.INTER_AREA)

cv2.imwrite("compressed_image.jpg", compressed_image)
```

This AI model **reduces file size while preserving key visual details**, enhancing web performance.

---

3. AI-Driven Video Compression

Video content is **one of the largest data-consuming elements** on the web. AI-based video compression improves efficiency by:

- **Reducing bitrate intelligently without losing detail.**
- **Enhancing frame prediction and interpolation.**
- **Optimizing encoding for different network conditions.**

AI Video Optimization Technique	Function	Example Use Case
AI-Based Bitrate Reduction	Dynamically adjusts bitrate for smooth playback.	AI optimizing YouTube video streaming on slow networks.
Neural Network Super-Resolution	Enhances lower-quality videos to HD using AI.	AI improving Netflix playback quality on compressed files.

AI-Powered Frame Prediction	Reduces redundant frames to save bandwidth.	AI optimizing TikTok video uploads.
Automated Encoding Optimization	AI selects best encoding formats dynamically.	AI-driven adaptive streaming in Amazon Prime Video.

By integrating **AI-based compression techniques**, websites can **reduce bandwidth consumption and improve media-rich web performance.**

Machine Learning for Predicting Server Load

1. The Importance of AI in Server Load Prediction

High traffic surges can **overload web servers**, causing slow performance or downtime. AI-powered **server load prediction models** analyze:

- **User traffic patterns.**
- **CPU, RAM, and bandwidth utilization.**
- **Peak usage times and historical data.**

By predicting server load in advance, AI can **dynamically allocate resources, auto-scale servers, and prevent downtime.**

---

2. AI Techniques for Server Load Prediction

AI Model	Function	Example Use Case
Time-Series Forecasting	Predicts future server demand based on historical usage.	AI anticipating Black Friday traffic spikes.

Reinforcement Learning for Load Balancing	AI optimizes server traffic distribution.	AI preventing cloud server overload.
Predictive Auto-Scaling	Adjusts cloud resources dynamically.	AWS Lambda AI auto-scaling based on real-time load.
Anomaly Detection for Traffic Spikes	AI detects unusual traffic patterns and prevents failures.	AI blocking bot-driven traffic surges.

---

3. Implementing AI for Server Load Prediction

Example: Using AI to Predict Server Load with Python

python

CopyEdit

```
import pandas as pd

from sklearn.ensemble import RandomForestRegressor

from sklearn.model_selection import train_test_split


# Load server traffic data

data = pd.read_csv("server_load.csv")


# Define features and target variable

X = data[['CPU_Usage', 'RAM_Usage', 'Network_Traffic']]

y = data['Server_Load']
```

```
# Train AI model

X_train, X_test, y_train, y_test = train_test_split(X, y,
test_size=0.2)

model = RandomForestRegressor()

model.fit(X_train, y_train)


# Predict future server load

future_load = model.predict([[70, 16, 100]])  # Example inputs

print(f"Predicted Server Load: {future_load}")
```

This AI model **analyzes past server metrics and predicts future load**, helping **prevent server crashes and optimize resource allocation**.

AI-powered performance optimization **enhances web speed, media compression, and server scalability**. By leveraging AI-driven **CDNs, search preloading, lazy loading, and predictive auto-scaling**, businesses **reduce latency, optimize resources, and ensure seamless user experiences**.

Future developments in **AI-based performance optimization** will include:

- **Deep learning models for real-time web speed analysis**.
- **AI-powered 5G optimization for web and mobile networks**.
- **Edge computing combined with AI for ultra-fast data processing**.

By integrating AI into **web performance strategies**, businesses can **improve user retention, boost SEO rankings, and enhance overall digital experiences**.

Chapter 11

AI in Cloud and Serverless Web Development

AI-Powered DevOps for CI/CD Automation

Introduction to AI in DevOps and CI/CD

Continuous Integration (CI) and Continuous Deployment (CD) are fundamental in modern DevOps workflows, enabling **rapid software development, testing, and deployment**. However, managing CI/CD pipelines manually can lead to **configuration errors, deployment failures, and inefficiencies**.

AI-powered DevOps enhances **automation, security, and efficiency** by:

- **Predicting and preventing deployment failures.**
- **Optimizing infrastructure management.**
- **Automating error detection and resolution.**
- **Enhancing resource allocation for cloud services.**

By integrating **Machine Learning (ML), AI-driven monitoring, and predictive analytics**, organizations can **improve software delivery, reduce downtime, and enhance system reliability**.

---

1. AI-Powered CI/CD Automation Techniques

AI-Driven CI/CD Feature	Function	Example Use Case
AI-Based Test Automation	AI automatically detects **code changes and runs necessary tests**.	AI optimizing **unit testing in a microservices architecture**.

Predictive Deployment Failures	AI predicts **failed deployments before they happen**.	AI preventing **misconfigured Kubernetes pods from being deployed**.
AI-Powered Log Analysis	AI scans logs in real time to **detect anomalies in build processes**.	AI identifying **memory leaks in cloud applications**.
AI-Driven Resource Optimization	AI adjusts CI/CD pipeline resources **based on demand**.	AI scaling **AWS EC2 instances dynamically**.

---

2. AI in Continuous Integration (CI)

How AI Enhances CI Pipelines:

- **Smart Code Analysis** → AI-powered tools like **DeepCode and GitHub Copilot** analyze pull requests, detect vulnerabilities, and suggest improvements.
- **Automated Build Optimization** → AI dynamically adjusts **build processes**, improving **compilation speed and error detection**.
- **Predictive Test Execution** → AI identifies **which test cases should run** based on recent changes, reducing **unnecessary test execution**.

Example: AI-Driven Continuous Integration Pipeline

yaml

CopyEdit

```
name: AI-Powered CI Pipeline


on:
```

118

```yaml
  push:
    branches:
      - main

jobs:
  build:
    runs-on: ubuntu-latest
    steps:
      - name: Checkout Code
        uses: actions/checkout@v2

      - name: Install Dependencies
        run: npm install

      - name: AI-Powered Code Analysis
        run: ai-linter analyze src/

      - name: Run Tests
        run: npm test

      - name: Deploy Application
        run: deploy.sh
```

This AI-enhanced pipeline **automatically detects issues, runs intelligent tests, and optimizes deployment**.

---

3. AI in Continuous Deployment (CD)

How AI Optimizes CD Pipelines:

- **AI-Powered Rollback Strategies** → AI detects **deployment failures in real time** and rolls back to a stable version.
- **Smart Deployment Schedules** → AI analyzes **traffic patterns** to deploy updates **at low-impact times**.
- **Predictive Security Checks** → AI scans **new releases for vulnerabilities** before deployment.

Example: AI-Enhanced Kubernetes Deployment Strategy

yaml

CopyEdit

```
apiVersion: apps/v1

kind: Deployment

metadata:

  name: web-app

spec:

  replicas: 3

  strategy:

    rollingUpdate:

      maxSurge: 1

      maxUnavailable: 1
```

120

```
template:
  metadata:
    labels:
      app: web
  spec:
    containers:
    - name: web
      image: ai-optimized-container:v1
      resources:
        limits:
          cpu: "500m"
          memory: "512Mi"
```

This configuration ensures **AI-powered resource allocation and fail-safe deployments**.

Leveraging AI in AWS, Google Cloud, and Azure AI

1. AI-Powered Cloud Services Overview

Major cloud providers—**AWS, Google Cloud, and Azure**—offer AI-powered services for **machine learning, automation, and web application enhancement**.

Cloud Provide r	AI-Powered Services	Use Case

AWS	AWS SageMaker, AI-powered Auto Scaling, AI-enhanced security (GuardDuty)	AI-driven **image recognition and fraud detection**
Google Cloud	AutoML, Vertex AI, AI-powered BigQuery analytics	AI-powered **search and natural language processing**
Azure	Azure Cognitive Services, AI-powered anomaly detection	AI-based **sentiment analysis and predictive analytics**

2. AI in AWS Cloud Services

AWS offers AI-powered services that **enhance application scalability, security, and performance**:

Key AWS AI Services

AWS AI Service	Function	Example Use Case
Amazon SageMaker	Trains and deploys ML models automatically.	AI-powered **fraud detection in banking applications**.
AWS Lambda AI	Automates serverless computing with AI-enhanced execution.	AI-driven **image processing for mobile applications**.
AWS GuardDuty	Uses AI to detect **security threats in AWS environments**.	AI monitoring **cloud-based API attacks**.

Example: AI-Driven AWS Auto Scaling

json

CopyEdit

```json
{
  "AutoScalingGroupName": "web-app-autoscaling",
  "MinSize": 2,
  "MaxSize": 10,
  "TargetTrackingConfiguration": {
    "PredefinedMetricSpecification": {
      "PredefinedMetricType": "ASGCPUUtilization"
    },
    "TargetValue": 50.0
  }
}
```

This configuration ensures **AI-driven auto-scaling based on server demand**.

---

3. AI in Google Cloud Services

Google Cloud provides **AI-powered automation, data processing, and NLP capabilities**.

123

Key Google Cloud AI Services

Google Cloud AI Service	Function	Example Use Case
Vertex AI	Automates ML model deployment and training.	AI-enhanced **medical diagnosis predictions**.
BigQuery ML	AI-powered SQL-based machine learning.	AI-driven **real-time fraud detection in banking**.
Cloud AutoML	AI-based model training for developers without ML expertise.	AI-powered **recommendation engines**.

4. AI in Microsoft Azure Cloud Services

Azure provides **enterprise-grade AI solutions** for **image recognition, anomaly detection, and natural language processing**.

Key Azure AI Services

Azure AI Service	Function	Example Use Case
Azure Cognitive Services	AI-driven **speech, vision, and language processing**.	AI-powered **real-time chat translations**.
Azure AI Anomaly Detector	AI detects **unusual patterns in time-series data**.	AI-powered **financial fraud detection**.

124

Integrating AI in Serverless Web Applications

1. AI-Powered Serverless Architectures

Serverless web development allows applications to **run without managing infrastructure**, while AI enhances serverless computing by:

- **Auto-scaling workloads efficiently.**
- **Predicting API traffic fluctuations.**
- **Optimizing database queries dynamically.**

---

2. AI-Driven Serverless Workflows

AI-Powered Serverless Feature	Function	Example Use Case
AI-Optimized API Gateway	AI enhances **API request routing.**	AI **predicting API usage spikes** and pre-scaling resources.
Event-Driven AI Processing	AI **triggers serverless functions based on user actions.**	AI **automatically analyzing uploaded images in cloud storage.**
Auto-Scaling AI-Powered Databases	AI adjusts **NoSQL or SQL performance** dynamically.	AI optimizing **Firestore** queries in real-time applications.

Example: AI-Driven AWS Lambda Serverless Function

python

CopyEdit

125

```python
import json

import boto3


def lambda_handler(event, context):

    # AI-Powered Sentiment Analysis

    comprehend = boto3.client("comprehend")

    response = comprehend.detect_sentiment(Text=event["text"],
LanguageCode="en")


    return {"Sentiment": response["Sentiment"]}
```

This AI-powered serverless function **analyzes text sentiment dynamically**.

AI in **cloud and serverless development** enhances **DevOps automation, resource optimization, security, and performance**. By leveraging **AI-powered CI/CD, cloud computing, and auto-scaling**, businesses can build **scalable, efficient, and intelligent web applications**.

Future developments will include:

- **AI-optimized Kubernetes clusters** for fully autonomous cloud orchestration.
- **Serverless AI-driven event streaming** for real-time applications.
- **Predictive AI-based security automation** in cloud environments.

By integrating **AI into cloud and serverless web development**, businesses can **reduce costs, improve efficiency, and deliver smarter applications**.

Chapter 12

Ethical Considerations and Challenges in AI Web Development

Bias and Fairness in AI Web Applications

Introduction to Bias in AI

AI-powered web applications **automate decision-making, personalize user experiences, and enhance efficiency**, but they also introduce the risk of **bias and unfair treatment**. AI systems are trained on large datasets, and **if these datasets contain historical biases, the AI model can perpetuate or amplify them.**

Bias in AI can lead to:

- **Unfair treatment of certain user groups.**
- **Discrimination in automated decision-making (e.g., hiring, lending, recommendation systems).**
- **Reinforcement of stereotypes in content generation and moderation.**

Addressing bias is critical to ensuring **fair, inclusive, and ethical AI-powered web applications.**

---

1. How Bias Appears in AI Web Applications

Type of Bias	Description	Example
Data Bias	AI models trained on **imbalanced datasets** reflect the **dominant group's preferences** while marginalizing others.	AI-based resume screening favoring male applicants due to historical hiring patterns.

Algorith mic Bias	Machine learning models **reinforce societal biases** during training.	AI image recognition misclassifying people based on race.
Selectio n Bias	Data collected **does not represent the full diversity of users**.	AI chatbot trained only on English text, leading to poor multilingual support.
Automat ion Bias	Over-reliance on AI-generated decisions without human oversight.	AI-powered loan approval rejecting qualified applicants unfairly.

---

2. Addressing Bias in AI Web Development

a) Using Diverse and Representative Training Data

- **Ensure datasets include diverse demographics, languages, and user behaviors**.
- **Balance data distribution** to avoid over-representation of certain groups.

b) Implementing Fair AI Algorithms

- Use **bias detection tools** like IBM AI Fairness 360 and Google's What-If Tool.
- Apply **differential privacy techniques** to prevent discrimination in AI models.

c) Conducting Regular Bias Audits

- Periodically **evaluate AI model outcomes for disparities**.
- Incorporate **human oversight in AI decision-making**.

d) Transparency and Explainability in AI Models

- Provide **clear explanations** for AI-driven decisions.
- Allow **users to challenge AI predictions or recommendations**.

Example: AI Fairness in Hiring Applications

If an AI hiring tool consistently **favors male applicants**, developers should:

- **Train the AI on diverse candidate data.**
- **Use fairness-aware algorithms that neutralize gender bias.**
- **Provide candidates with explanations and appeal mechanisms.**

By addressing bias, AI web applications **become more ethical, inclusive, and trustworthy**.

Privacy and Security Concerns in AI-Powered Websites

1. Privacy Risks in AI-Powered Web Applications

AI-driven websites collect **large volumes of personal data** for:

- **Personalized recommendations.**
- **Targeted advertising.**
- **User behavior analysis.**

Without proper safeguards, **AI-powered web applications can compromise user privacy**.

Major AI Privacy Concerns

Privacy Issue	Description	Example
Data Collection Without Consent	AI **tracks user behavior** without explicit permission.	AI analyzing **mouse movements and keystrokes without user knowledge**.
Excessive Data Retention	AI models store **unnecessary user**	AI-driven chatbots **storing conversations indefinitely**.

	data, increasing privacy risks.	
AI-Based User Profiling	AI categorizes users based on their behavior, sometimes inaccurately.	AI identifying **users' political or religious views through content interactions**.
Facial Recognition and Biometric Data Risks	AI-powered **face recognition systems can be misused** for surveillance.	AI storing and recognizing faces **without user permission**.

2. AI-Powered Security Risks

Security Concern	How It Happens	Example
Adversarial Attacks on AI Models	Hackers manipulate **AI models by injecting deceptive inputs**.	AI image recognition misclassifying **objects due to subtle pixel modifications**.
AI-Powered Phishing and Fraud	Cybercriminals use AI to **generate realistic phishing emails and deepfake videos**.	AI creating **fraudulent customer support chatbots to steal data**.
Data Leakage from AI Models	AI models inadvertently reveal **sensitive training data**.	AI chatbots **leaking private user conversations**.

3. Mitigating Privacy and Security Risks in AI Web Applications

a) Privacy-Focused AI Design

- Implement **data minimization strategies** (collect only necessary data).
- Use **federated learning** to train AI models without accessing raw user data.
- Ensure **AI-driven tracking and profiling comply with consent laws**.

b) Strengthening AI Security Measures

- Employ **AI-driven anomaly detection** to identify suspicious activities.
- Secure AI models against **adversarial attacks**.
- Encrypt AI training datasets to prevent **data leakage**.

c) User Control and Transparency

- Allow users to **opt out of AI tracking**.
- Provide **clear privacy policies explaining AI usage**.
- Enable **data deletion requests and AI explainability tools**.

Example: AI Privacy in Smart Assistants

AI-powered assistants like **Alexa and Google Assistant** have faced scrutiny for **storing voice recordings**. Ethical AI design ensures:

- **Users can delete recorded data.**
- **Voice recognition AI operates only with explicit permission.**
- **Conversations remain end-to-end encrypted.**

By addressing **AI privacy and security risks**, web applications **gain user trust and meet legal compliance standards**.

Compliance with GDPR, CCPA, and Other Regulations

1. Key AI Privacy Regulations

Regulation	Scope	AI Impact

GDPR (General Data Protection Regulation - EU)	Covers **data privacy rights and AI transparency**.	AI must obtain **explicit consent before data collection**.
CCPA (California Consumer Privacy Act - USA)	Protects **California residents from AI-driven tracking**.	Users can **opt out of AI profiling** and request data deletion.
AI Act (European Union - Proposed)	Regulates **high-risk AI applications**.	AI systems **must be transparent and explainable**.
PIPEDA (Canada)	Ensures **fair AI-driven data processing**.	AI-powered decisions **must be auditable**.

2. Ensuring AI Compliance in Web Applications

a) Data Transparency & User Consent

- Clearly **disclose AI usage in privacy policies**.
- Implement **opt-in mechanisms for AI-powered personalization**.

b) AI Explainability & Auditability

- Provide users with **explanations for AI decisions**.
- Maintain **records of AI-driven data processing**.

c) Data Access and Deletion Rights

- Allow users to **view, edit, and delete their AI-stored data**.
- Ensure AI systems comply with **"Right to be Forgotten" laws**.

Example: GDPR Compliance in AI-Powered E-Commerce

A European e-commerce platform using AI-driven recommendations must:

- **Inform users how AI analyzes their browsing data.**
- **Allow users to opt out of AI personalization.**
- **Delete user data upon request.**

By adhering to **GDPR, CCPA, and global privacy laws**, AI-powered websites **avoid legal penalties and build trust with users**.

Ethical AI web development requires:

- **Fair and unbiased AI models** that promote inclusivity.
- **Privacy-first AI architectures** that respect user data rights.
- **Security-focused AI solutions** that prevent fraud, hacking, and abuse.
- **Compliance with global regulations (GDPR, CCPA, AI Act, etc.)** to protect user interests.

By addressing **bias, privacy risks, and regulatory compliance**, AI-powered web applications can **enhance innovation while ensuring ethical responsibility**.

Chapter 13

Building an AI-Powered Chatbot for a Website

Designing a Chatbot Using OpenAI and Python/JavaScript

Introduction to AI-Powered Chatbots

Chatbots have become a fundamental part of modern web applications, **automating customer support, improving engagement, and streamlining interactions**. AI-powered chatbots use **Natural Language Processing (NLP), Machine Learning (ML), and deep learning algorithms** to provide **human-like responses**.

Using **OpenAI's GPT-4, Python, and JavaScript**, developers can build **intelligent chatbots that understand context, process user queries, and deliver dynamic responses**.

---

1. Understanding Chatbot Architecture

AI chatbots consist of the following core components:

Component	Function	Example Use Case
NLP Engine	Processes user queries and extracts meaning.	OpenAI's GPT-4, Google Dialogflow.

Intent Recognitio n	Identifies user intent from the message.	AI detects **"book a flight"** as a booking request.
Response Generator	Uses AI models to generate human-like replies.	GPT-4 generating dynamic responses.
Integration Layer	Connects chatbot to a website, database, or APIs.	JavaScript embedding chatbot on a website.

2. Implementing an AI Chatbot with OpenAI and Python

Step 1: Install Dependencies

First, install the required libraries:

bash

CopyEdit

```
pip install openai flask requests
```

Step 2: Set Up a Flask API for the Chatbot

python

CopyEdit

```
from flask import Flask, request, jsonify

import openai

import os
```

```python
app = Flask(__name__)


# Load API key

openai.api_key = os.getenv("OPENAI_API_KEY")


@app.route("/chatbot", methods=["POST"])

def chatbot():

    user_message = request.json["message"]


    # AI Model Call

    response = openai.ChatCompletion.create(

        model="gpt-4",

        messages=[{"role": "user", "content": user_message}]

    )


    return jsonify({"reply":
response["choices"][0]["message"]["content"]})


if __name__ == "__main__":

    app.run(port=5000, debug=True)
```

This Flask API processes **user input, sends it to OpenAI, and returns an AI-generated response**.

3. Implementing a Chatbot Front-End with JavaScript

Step 1: Create an HTML Front-End for the Chatbot

html

CopyEdit

```html
<!DOCTYPE html>
<html lang="en">
<head>
    <title>AI Chatbot</title>
    <script>
        async function sendMessage() {
            const userInput =
document.getElementById("userInput").value;

            const response = await fetch("/chatbot", {
                method: "POST",
                headers: { "Content-Type": "application/json"
},
                body: JSON.stringify({ message: userInput })
            });

            const data = await response.json();

            document.getElementById("chat").innerHTML +=
`<p>User: ${userInput}</p><p>Bot: ${data.reply}</p>`;

        }

    </script>
</head>
```

```
<body>

    <h1>AI Chatbot</h1>

    <div id="chat"></div>

    <input type="text" id="userInput" placeholder="Type a
message">

    <button onclick="sendMessage()">Send</button>

</body>

</html>
```

This simple interface **sends user input to the Flask API** and displays the
AI-generated responses.

Deploying the Chatbot in a Web Application

1. Hosting the Flask API on a Cloud Server

To deploy the chatbot, use a **cloud service like AWS, Google Cloud, or Heroku**.

Deploying on Heroku

Install Heroku CLI:
 bash
CopyEdit
```
npm install -g heroku
```

   1.

Initialize a Heroku project:
 bash
CopyEdit
```
heroku create my-chatbot-app
```

   2.

Deploy the Flask app:
bash
CopyEdit

```
git add .

git commit -m "Deploy chatbot"

git push heroku main
```

 3.

Scale the chatbot API:
bash
CopyEdit

```
heroku ps:scale web=1
```

 4.

Now, the chatbot API is **publicly available and ready to integrate into any website**.

---

2. Embedding the Chatbot in a Website

To integrate the chatbot into an existing web application, use **JavaScript and WebSockets for real-time interactions**.

Embedding the Chatbot in a Web Page

html

CopyEdit

```
<script>
    async function chatWithBot() {

        let userMessage =
document.getElementById("userMessage").value;

        let response = await
fetch("https://my-chatbot-app.herokuapp.com/chatbot", {
```

```
        method: "POST",

        headers: { "Content-Type": "application/json" },

        body: JSON.stringify({ message: userMessage })

    });

    let data = await response.json();

    document.getElementById("chatbox").innerHTML +=
`<p>User: ${userMessage}</p><p>Bot: ${data.reply}</p>`;

    }

</script>
```

This JavaScript script **fetches responses from the deployed chatbot API and displays them dynamically**.

Enhancing the Chatbot with Machine Learning

1. Improving Chatbot Responses with NLP

To enhance chatbot capabilities, **machine learning models can refine understanding, intent recognition, and contextual awareness.**

ML Enhancem ent	Function	Example
Sentiment Analysis	Detects user emotions and adjusts responses.	AI chatbot **providing empathetic responses to frustrated users**.

Context Retention	Remembers previous interactions for better flow.	AI **continuing conversations seamlessly**.
Intent Classification	Detects what users want (e.g., booking, FAQs).	AI identifying **whether a query is a complaint or a request**.

Example: Adding Sentiment Analysis to the Chatbot

python

CopyEdit

```
from textblob import TextBlob


@app.route("/chatbot", methods=["POST"])

def chatbot():

    user_message = request.json["message"]

    sentiment = TextBlob(user_message).sentiment.polarity


    response = openai.ChatCompletion.create(

        model="gpt-4",

        messages=[{"role": "user", "content": user_message}]

    )


    ai_reply = response["choices"][0]["message"]["content"]
```

```python
    if sentiment < 0:

        ai_reply += " I see that you're upset. How can I
assist you better?"


    return jsonify({"reply": ai_reply})
```

This enhancement **modifies chatbot responses based on user sentiment**, creating **a more engaging and emotionally aware chatbot**.

---

2. Training a Custom Machine Learning Model for Chatbot Enhancements

For businesses requiring a **domain-specific chatbot**, a custom-trained model using **TensorFlow or PyTorch** can improve accuracy.

Training an AI Model with Intent Recognition

python

CopyEdit

```python
from sklearn.feature_extraction.text import CountVectorizer

from sklearn.linear_model import LogisticRegression


# Sample chatbot training data

training_data = [

    ("What are your business hours?", "business_hours"),

    ("How do I reset my password?", "password_reset"),

    ("Tell me a joke!", "joke"),
```

```
]

# Preparing training dataset
X_train, y_train = zip(*training_data)
vectorizer = CountVectorizer()
X_train_vectors = vectorizer.fit_transform(X_train)

# Training intent classification model
model = LogisticRegression()
model.fit(X_train_vectors, y_train)

# Predict user intent
def predict_intent(user_input):
    user_vector = vectorizer.transform([user_input])
    return model.predict(user_vector)[0]

# Example
print(predict_intent("What time do you open?"))  # Expected
output: "business_hours"
```

This model classifies **user intent** and helps the chatbot **respond more accurately.**

By combining **OpenAI's GPT-4, Python, JavaScript, and machine learning**, developers can build **intelligent, scalable, and adaptive chatbots** for web applications.

Key takeaways:

- **AI-powered chatbots improve user experience and automate customer service.**
- **Deploying chatbots in the cloud ensures high availability and scalability.**
- **Enhancements like sentiment analysis and intent recognition create more intelligent chatbots.**

With further advancements in **NLP, deep learning, and AI automation**, chatbots will **continue evolving into highly interactive virtual assistants for businesses and users worldwide**.

Chapter 14

Implementing AI-Based Image Recognition in a Web App

Using TensorFlow.js for Image Classification

Introduction to AI-Based Image Recognition

Image recognition is one of the most transformative AI applications in web development. AI-powered image recognition allows web applications to **classify, detect, and process visual data** in real time. This capability enhances **user experience, security, accessibility, and automation**.

TensorFlow.js, an open-source JavaScript library, enables **on-device machine learning for image classification directly in the browser** without requiring a backend server. This makes it an ideal choice for **fast, scalable, and privacy-friendly image recognition applications**.

---

1. What is TensorFlow.js?

TensorFlow.js is a **JavaScript version of TensorFlow**, allowing developers to:

- **Run AI models directly in a web browser** (reducing server load).
- **Train and fine-tune models in real-time**.
- **Integrate AI-powered image recognition into websites and web apps**.

Advantages of Using TensorFlow.js for Image Classification

Feature	Benefit
Runs on the client-side	No need for cloud-based inference, ensuring

	faster processing and better privacy.
Supports pre-trained models	Developers can **use existing image recognition models** instead of training from scratch.
Works on all devices	Runs on **mobile and desktop browsers** without installing extra software.

---

2. Implementing Image Classification with TensorFlow.js

Step 1: Set Up TensorFlow.js in an HTML Web Page

Add TensorFlow.js to your web project:

html

CopyEdit

```
<script
src="https://cdn.jsdelivr.net/npm/@tensorflow/tfjs"></script>

<script
src="https://cdn.jsdelivr.net/npm/@tensorflow-models/mobilenet
"></script>
```

Step 2: Create an HTML Page for Image Upload

html

CopyEdit

146

```
<!DOCTYPE html>

<html lang="en">

<head>

    <title>AI Image Recognition</title>

</head>

<body>

    <h1>Upload an Image for AI Recognition</h1>

    <input type="file" id="imageInput" accept="image/*">

    <img id="previewImage" width="300">

    <p id="result"></p>


    <script>

        async function classifyImage() {

            const image =
document.getElementById("previewImage");

            const model = await mobilenet.load();

            const predictions = await model.classify(image);

            document.getElementById("result").innerText =
`Prediction: ${predictions[0].className}`;

        }


document.getElementById("imageInput").addEventListener("change
", function(event) {
```
147

```
            const file = event.target.files[0];

            const reader = new FileReader();

            reader.onload = function() {

                    document.getElementById("previewImage").src =
reader.result;

                    setTimeout(classifyImage, 500); // Delay to
allow image loading

            };

            reader.readAsDataURL(file);

        });

    </script>

</body>

</html>
```

How It Works

- Users **upload an image**.
- TensorFlow.js **loads a pre-trained MobileNet model**.
- AI **analyzes the image and predicts the object category**.

Expected Output: If a user uploads a picture of a dog, the output might be:

makefile

CopyEdit

```
Prediction: Labrador Retriever
```

This method enables **real-time AI image classification** without **requiring a backend server**.

148

Deploying an AI-Powered Image Recognition Tool on a Website

1. Hosting the Web App on GitHub Pages, Netlify, or Firebase

Once the image classification tool is ready, it needs to be **deployed on a web server**.

Deploying on GitHub Pages

1. **Push your project to GitHub**.
2. In your repository, go to **Settings > Pages**.
3. Choose the **main branch and root directory** for deployment.

Deploying on Firebase Hosting

Install Firebase CLI:
 bash
CopyEdit
```
npm install -g firebase-tools
```

1.

Initialize Firebase in your project:
 bash
CopyEdit
```
firebase init
```

2.

Deploy the web app:
 bash
CopyEdit
```
firebase deploy
```

3.

Once deployed, users can **upload images and receive AI-generated classifications directly from their browser**.

149

2. Enhancing Image Recognition with a Custom Model

For **more accurate domain-specific image recognition**, TensorFlow.js allows **training custom models**.

Example: Training an AI Model for Plant Disease Detection

javascript

CopyEdit

```javascript
import * as tf from '@tensorflow/tfjs';


// Load dataset
const dataset = await tf.data.csv('plant_disease_data.csv');


// Define model
const model = tf.sequential();
model.add(tf.layers.conv2d({filters: 32, kernelSize: 3,
activation: 'relu', inputShape: [128, 128, 3]}));
model.add(tf.layers.flatten());
model.add(tf.layers.dense({units: 128, activation: 'relu'}));
model.add(tf.layers.dense({units: 5, activation: 'softmax'}));


// Train model
await model.compile({optimizer: 'adam', loss:
'categoricalCrossentropy', metrics: ['accuracy']});
await model.fit(dataset, {epochs: 10});
```

150

```
// Save the model

await model.save('downloads://plant-disease-model');
```

This allows web apps to **classify plant diseases** using **AI-powered detection**.

Enhancing Web Security with AI-Based Facial Recognition

1. AI-Powered Face Recognition for Authentication

Facial recognition enhances **web security** by:

- **Replacing traditional logins with AI-powered facial authentication.**
- **Preventing identity fraud by detecting deepfakes and spoofing attacks.**
- **Restricting unauthorized access based on facial data.**

---

2. Implementing Facial Recognition with TensorFlow.js

Step 1: Add Face Detection Libraries

html

CopyEdit

```
<script
src="https://cdn.jsdelivr.net/npm/@tensorflow/tfjs"></script>

<script
src="https://cdn.jsdelivr.net/npm/@tensorflow-models/blazeface"></script>
```

Step 2: Create a Face Recognition System

html

CopyEdit

```html
<!DOCTYPE html>

<html lang="en">

<head>

    <title>AI Face Recognition</title>

</head>

<body>

    <h1>Face Detection with AI</h1>

    <video id="video" width="320" height="240"
autoplay></video>

    <canvas id="canvas"></canvas>

    <p id="status"></p>


    <script>

        async function detectFaces() {

            const video = document.getElementById("video");

            const model = await blazeface.load();

            const predictions = await
model.estimateFaces(video, false);


            if (predictions.length > 0) {

                document.getElementById("status").innerText =
"Face Detected!";
```

152

```
                } else {

                    document.getElementById("status").innerText =
"No Face Detected.";

                }

            }


        // Start camera

        navigator.mediaDevices.getUserMedia({ video: true })

            .then(stream => {

                document.getElementById("video").srcObject =
stream;

                setInterval(detectFaces, 500);

            });

    </script>

</body>

</html>
```

How It Works:

- Uses **BlazeFace (an AI face detection model)** to analyze a live camera feed.
- Detects if a **face is present** and updates the status.

Enhancements: AI-Powered Facial Authentication

- Integrate with **FaceNet for identity verification**.
- Use AI to detect **fake faces or deepfakes**.
- Store encrypted **face embeddings** for secure authentication.

153

AI-powered image recognition is **revolutionizing web applications**, enabling:

1. **Real-time object classification with TensorFlow.js**.
2. **AI-powered image recognition tools for e-commerce, security, and accessibility**.
3. **AI-enhanced facial authentication for web security**.

Future advancements include:

- **AI-driven OCR (Optical Character Recognition) for extracting text from images**.
- **Neural networks for object tracking in live video feeds**.
- **Edge AI computing to run AI models directly on user devices**.

By integrating **AI-based image recognition**, developers can create **powerful, intelligent, and secure web applications**.

Chapter 15

Creating an AI-Powered Recommendation System

Building a Personalized Recommendation Engine

Introduction to AI-Powered Recommendation Systems

Recommendation systems are essential for **enhancing user engagement, increasing sales, and providing personalized experiences** on websites. AI-driven recommendation engines **analyze user behavior, preferences, and historical interactions** to suggest relevant content, products, or services.

Modern recommendation engines utilize **Machine Learning (ML), Deep Learning, and Natural Language Processing (NLP)** to make **accurate, dynamic, and personalized recommendations**.

---

1. Types of AI-Based Recommendation Systems

Type	Description	Example Use Case
Content-Based Filtering	Recommends items similar to past interactions.	Netflix suggesting movies based on past watch history.
Collaborative Filtering	Analyzes behaviors of similar users to make recommendations.	Amazon recommending products based on customers with similar purchase history.

Hybrid Systems	Combines **content-based and collaborative filtering** for better accuracy.	Spotify suggesting music based on listening history and similar users.
Deep Learning-Based Recommendati ons	Uses neural networks to predict **complex user preferences**.	YouTube personalizing video suggestions based on deep learning models.

---

2. Implementing a Personalized Recommendation Engine Using Python

A basic recommendation engine can be implemented using **collaborative filtering and content-based filtering**.

Step 1: Install Dependencies

bash

CopyEdit

```
pip install pandas numpy scikit-learn
```

Step 2: Load and Prepare Data

python

CopyEdit

```
import pandas as pd

from sklearn.feature_extraction.text import TfidfVectorizer

from sklearn.metrics.pairwise import cosine_similarity
```

```python
# Sample product dataset
data = {
    "ProductID": [1, 2, 3, 4],
    "ProductName": ["Wireless Headphones", "Bluetooth
Speaker", "Smartwatch", "Noise-Canceling Headphones"],
    "Category": ["Audio", "Audio", "Wearables", "Audio"],
    "Description": ["Over-ear headphones with deep bass",
                    "Portable speaker with Bluetooth 5.0",
                    "Fitness tracker with heart rate
monitoring",
                    "Premium headphones with active noise
cancellation"]
}


df = pd.DataFrame(data)


# Convert text descriptions into numerical features
vectorizer = TfidfVectorizer(stop_words="english")
tfidf_matrix = vectorizer.fit_transform(df["Description"])


# Compute similarity between products
cosine_sim = cosine_similarity(tfidf_matrix)
```

Step 3: Create a Recommendation Function

python

CopyEdit

```python
def recommend_products(product_name, df, similarity_matrix):
    index = df[df["ProductName"] == product_name].index[0]
    similar_products = list(enumerate(similarity_matrix[index]))
    similar_products = sorted(similar_products, key=lambda x: x[1], reverse=True)[1:3]


    recommended_products = [df.iloc[i[0]]["ProductName"] for i in similar_products]
    return recommended_products


# Example: Recommend products similar to "Wireless Headphones"
print(recommend_products("Wireless Headphones", df, cosine_sim))
```

Expected Output:

css

CopyEdit

```css
['Noise-Canceling Headphones', 'Bluetooth Speaker']
```

This **content-based filtering model** finds similar products based on **text descriptions** and **feature similarity**.

Implementing AI Recommendations in E-Commerce Web Apps

1. Integrating AI Recommendations in an E-Commerce Platform

AI-driven recommendation engines help **e-commerce websites boost sales by providing personalized product suggestions**.

Recommendation Type	Function	Example Use Case
"Customers Also Bought"	Uses **collaborative filtering** to suggest products frequently bought together.	Amazon recommending complementary items in checkout.
"Recommended for You"	Analyzes user history to provide **personalized product suggestions**.	Netflix recommending personalized content based on watch history.
Trending Products	Uses real-time AI analytics to display **hot-selling products**.	AI-powered homepage recommendations based on trending searches.
Category-Based Recommendations	Suggests products **within a similar category**.	AI suggesting **fitness bands to users browsing smartwatches**.

2. Building an AI Recommendation API for E-Commerce

To integrate recommendations into an **e-commerce web app**, create an API that **dynamically suggests products**.

Step 1: Install Flask and Required Libraries

bash

CopyEdit

```
pip install flask numpy pandas scikit-learn
```

Step 2: Develop a Flask API for AI Recommendations

python

CopyEdit

```
from flask import Flask, request, jsonify

import pandas as pd

from sklearn.metrics.pairwise import cosine_similarity

from sklearn.feature_extraction.text import TfidfVectorizer


app = Flask(__name__)


# Sample product dataset
data = {
    "ProductID": [1, 2, 3, 4],
    "ProductName": ["Wireless Headphones", "Bluetooth Speaker", "Smartwatch", "Noise-Canceling Headphones"],
    "Description": ["Over-ear headphones with deep bass",
```

```python
                        "Portable speaker with Bluetooth 5.0",

                        "Fitness tracker with heart rate
monitoring",

                        "Premium headphones with active noise
cancellation"]
}


df = pd.DataFrame(data)


# Convert product descriptions into feature vectors
vectorizer = TfidfVectorizer(stop_words="english")
tfidf_matrix = vectorizer.fit_transform(df["Description"])
cosine_sim = cosine_similarity(tfidf_matrix)


# Define recommendation function
def get_recommendations(product_name):
    index = df[df["ProductName"] == product_name].index[0]
    similar_products = list(enumerate(cosine_sim[index]))
    similar_products = sorted(similar_products, key=lambda x:
x[1], reverse=True)[1:3]
    recommended_products = [df.iloc[i[0]]["ProductName"] for i
in similar_products]
    return recommended_products
```

```python
@app.route("/recommend", methods=["POST"])

def recommend():

    data = request.json

    product_name = data["product"]

    recommendations = get_recommendations(product_name)

    return jsonify({"recommended_products": recommendations})


if __name__ == "__main__":

    app.run(port=5000, debug=True)
```

Step 3: Connect AI API to a Web Front-End

html

CopyEdit

```html
<script>

    async function getRecommendations() {

        let product =
document.getElementById("productInput").value;

        let response = await
fetch("http://localhost:5000/recommend", {

            method: "POST",

            headers: { "Content-Type": "application/json" },

            body: JSON.stringify({ product: product })

        });
```

```
    let data = await response.json();

    document.getElementById("output").innerText =
`Recommended Products: ${data.recommended_products.join(",
")}`;

  }

</script>


<input type="text" id="productInput" placeholder="Enter
product name">

<button onclick="getRecommendations()">Get
Recommendations</button>

<p id="output"></p>
```

This AI-powered recommendation API **integrates with any e-commerce platform**, suggesting **relevant products to users dynamically**.

Testing and Optimizing AI-Powered Recommendations

1. Evaluating Recommendation Accuracy

To **measure the effectiveness of AI recommendations**, test using **metrics like precision, recall, and Mean Average Precision (MAP)**.

Example: Testing Recommendation Performance

python

CopyEdit

```
from sklearn.metrics import precision_score
```

```python
# Example of actual vs recommended products

actual_purchases = ["Wireless Headphones", "Smartwatch"]

recommended = ["Noise-Canceling Headphones", "Smartwatch"]


# Convert to binary format for precision calculation

actual_binary = [1 if item in actual_purchases else 0 for item in recommended]

recommended_binary = [1] * len(recommended)


precision = precision_score(actual_binary, recommended_binary)

print(f"Recommendation Precision: {precision:.2f}")
```

Precision Score Interpretation:

- **1.0** → Perfect recommendations.
- **0.5** → Half of the recommendations were relevant.
- **0.0** → Poor recommendations.

---

2. Optimizing AI Recommendations

Optimization Technique	Benefit
Personalization with Deep Learning	Uses user-specific embeddings for better recommendations.

Real-Time AI Adaptation	AI adjusts recommendations **based on current browsing behavior**.
Hybrid Filtering	Combines **content-based and collaborative filtering** for accuracy.

By **testing, fine-tuning, and optimizing AI recommendations**, businesses can boost engagement, increase conversions, and improve user experience.

AI-powered recommendation systems **enhance user engagement, improve e-commerce sales, and create a personalized browsing experience.** By integrating **machine learning, deep learning, and collaborative filtering,** developers can build **intelligent, data-driven recommendation engines** that adapt to user preferences in real-time.

Chapter 16

Automating SEO with AI

Using AI for Automated Keyword Analysis

Introduction to AI-Powered SEO

Search Engine Optimization (SEO) is essential for ensuring **higher rankings on search engines, improving visibility, and increasing organic traffic.** However, traditional SEO methods involve **manual keyword research, content optimization, and performance tracking,** which can be **time-consuming and inefficient.**

AI-powered SEO tools use **machine learning, natural language processing (NLP), and automation** to:

- Identify **high-impact keywords dynamically.**
- Analyze **search intent for better content alignment.**
- Optimize **website structure and content recommendations.**
- Enhance **metadata and link-building strategies.**

By leveraging **AI-based keyword analysis and automation,** businesses can improve their **SEO efficiency, reduce workload, and maximize search visibility.**

---

1. AI Techniques for Keyword Analysis

AI SEO Feature	Function	Example Use Case
AI-Based Keyword Extraction	Analyzes content and extracts **high-ranking keywords**.	AI scanning competitor blogs for **trending keywords**.

Intent-Based Keyword Matching	Determines **user search intent** (informational, commercial, transactional).	AI optimizing **product descriptions based on buyer intent**.
Predictive Keyword Ranking	AI predicts **which keywords will perform best over time**.	AI forecasting **seasonal keywords for e-commerce**.
AI-Generated Long-Tail Keywords	Finds **low-competition, high-conversion phrases**.	AI suggesting **"best budget wireless headphones for travel"** instead of generic "headphones".

---

2. Implementing AI for Keyword Analysis

Step 1: Install Required AI Libraries

bash

CopyEdit

```
pip install nltk pandas requests beautifulsoup4
```

Step 2: AI-Based Keyword Extraction Using NLP

python

CopyEdit

```
import nltk

from nltk.corpus import stopwords
```

```python
from collections import Counter

import requests

from bs4 import BeautifulSoup


nltk.download('stopwords')


def extract_keywords(url):
    # Scrape webpage content
    response = requests.get(url)
    soup = BeautifulSoup(response.text, "html.parser")
    text = soup.get_text()

    # Tokenize words
    words = text.lower().split()
    words = [word for word in words if word.isalpha() and word not in stopwords.words('english')]

    # Get most common keywords
    keyword_freq = Counter(words)
    return keyword_freq.most_common(10)


# Example usage: Analyze SEO of a webpage
print(extract_keywords("https://example.com"))
```

This AI model **automatically extracts the most relevant keywords from a webpage** for SEO optimization.

---

3. AI-Powered Keyword Intent Classification

AI can classify keywords into different **search intents**:

Search Intent	Description	Example
Informational	User is looking for knowledge.	"How does blockchain work?"
Navigational	User is looking for a specific website.	"OpenAI homepage"
Commercial	User is researching before purchasing.	"Best smartphones under $500"
Transactional	User intends to make a purchase.	"Buy iPhone 14 Pro online"

Example: AI for Keyword Intent Analysis

python

CopyEdit

```
from textblob import TextBlob


def classify_intent(keyword):
    blob = TextBlob(keyword)
```

169

```
if "how" in keyword or "what" in keyword:

    return "Informational"

elif "best" in keyword or "compare" in keyword:

    return "Commercial"

elif "buy" in keyword or "order" in keyword:

    return "Transactional"

else:

    return "Navigational"


# Example usage

print(classify_intent("Buy wireless headphones online"))   #
Output: Transactional
```

This AI-based classification **helps SEO teams optimize content for specific user intents**, increasing **conversion rates and search rankings**.

Developing an AI-Driven Web Performance Analyzer

1. The Role of AI in Web Performance Optimization

Website performance directly impacts **SEO rankings, user engagement, and conversion rates**. Google's ranking algorithms consider:

- **Page Load Speed**
- **Mobile-Friendliness**
- **Core Web Vitals (LCP, FID, CLS)**

AI-powered performance analyzers **detect inefficiencies and provide automated recommendations** for:

- Page speed optimization.
- Lazy loading and image compression.
- JavaScript and CSS minification.
- SEO-friendly UI improvements.

---

2. Implementing an AI Web Performance Analyzer

Step 1: Install Lighthouse for Web Performance Auditing

bash

CopyEdit

```
npm install -g lighthouse
```

Step 2: Run AI-Based Web Performance Analysis

bash

CopyEdit

```
lighthouse https://example.com --output=json
--output-path=report.json
```

This generates a **detailed SEO and performance report** for the given website.

Step 3: AI-Based Performance Optimization Suggestions

python

CopyEdit

```
import json


# Load Lighthouse report
```

171

```
with open("report.json") as file:

    data = json.load(file)


# Extract performance scores

performance_score = data["categories"]["performance"]["score"]

seo_score = data["categories"]["seo"]["score"]


# AI-Generated Suggestions

if performance_score < 0.7:

    print("Optimize images, remove unused CSS, enable lazy
loading.")

if seo_score < 0.8:

    print("Improve metadata, use structured data, optimize
page speed.")
```

This AI tool **automates performance checks and provides actionable recommendations for SEO improvements**.

Deploying an AI-Based SEO Optimization System

1. AI-Powered On-Page SEO Enhancements

AI Feature	Function	Example Use Case

AI-Based Meta Tag Optimization	Automatically generates **SEO-friendly titles and descriptions**.	AI creating **meta descriptions with high-ranking keywords**.
Automated Content Optimization	Enhances readability and keyword density.	AI suggesting **headline improvements for better ranking**.
Structured Data and Schema Markup	AI adds JSON-LD schema for **better indexing**.	AI structuring **product pages for rich snippets in Google**.

---

2. AI-Powered SEO Dashboard Development

To fully automate SEO optimization, an **AI-powered SEO dashboard** can monitor:

- **Keyword rankings over time.**
- **Traffic insights and conversion rates.**
- **SEO issues and AI-generated recommendations.**

Example: Building an AI SEO Dashboard with Python & Flask

python

CopyEdit

```
from flask import Flask, jsonify

import random


app = Flask(__name__)
```

```
@app.route("/seo_dashboard", methods=["GET"])

def seo_dashboard():

    data = {

        "page_speed_score": random.uniform(0.5, 1.0),

        "seo_score": random.uniform(0.6, 1.0),

        "top_keywords": ["AI SEO automation", "best AI tools
for SEO", "optimize website speed"],

        "recommendations": ["Compress images", "Improve
mobile-friendliness", "Add structured data"]

    }

    return jsonify(data)


if __name__ == "__main__":

    app.run(port=5000, debug=True)
```

This API **generates real-time SEO insights** for developers to integrate with a web dashboard.

AI-powered SEO automation enables:

1. **Automated keyword research and ranking analysis**.
2. **AI-driven web performance monitoring and speed optimization**.
3. **Dynamic SEO optimization tools for metadata, structured data, and content readability**.

Future advancements will include:

- **AI chatbots for real-time SEO recommendations**.
- **Deep learning for predicting SEO trends and algorithm changes**.
- **Voice search optimization using AI-based NLP**.

By integrating AI-driven SEO tools, businesses can **stay ahead of competition, improve search rankings, and drive organic traffic efficiently**.

www.ingramcontent.com/pod-product-compliance
Lightning Source LLC
La Vergne TN
LVHW022345060326
832902LV00022B/4257